Paul Bc
Peter Leve
Bill Ryan, Mich[illegible], Walter C. Veitsch, Doug Yurchey

Climategate
The Marijuana Conspiracy
Project Blue Beam
and other true stories from the Dot Connector magazine

Compiled by Paul Bondarovski

Text and cover design by Paul Bondarovski.

Illustrations:
title page – drawing by Paul Bondarovski;
p. 17 – by Paul Bondarovski (data courtesy of Michael Rivero);
pp. 9-10, 15 and 16 – courtesy of Michael Rivero;
p. 81 – taken from: *Evolution towards … the New Species*, by Ghis and Mado (Personocratia's Booklets, Booklet 1, 2008), used by permission;
pp. 118 and 124 – by Walter C. Vetsch, used by permission.

All articles (except *Introduction*) and illustrations have previously been published in the *Dot Connector* magazine (www.thedotconnector.org). See footnotes at the end of each article for details.

ISBN: 1451538146

Printed in the United States
First printing, March 2010

Contents

I give carte blanche to my Soul

Introduction

Paul Bondarovski

Something is wrong with the world... But you knew that! Otherwise you wouldn't be reading this book. You knew something was wrong, and you wanted to know what exactly. Press, television, and then Internet, never lacked explanations, analyses, indications, telling you that the System is damaged, that there are elements to replace, to repair, to improve. And they have been replaced, and repaired, and improved. Over and over again. Over and over – in vain... OK, nothing is perfect, you thought. But one day you had noticed something strange: the System improved, but – not the world. That was the day when you saw that the System and the world are not the same thing. That was the day you had woken up.

You have woken up, but still cannot see what exactly is wrong with the world. Because nothing has ever been wrong with the *real* world. What is wrong is the *virtual* world, like the wool pulled over your eyes by the System to blind you. The more you invest yourself, your forces and talents into repairing and improving that virtual world – the more you improve the System, and the more you help it to better blind and enslave you.

The System is not a kind of divine superpower. It is neither above you nor elsewhere outside of you – it is inside ... well, not of you, but of what it made you believe you are. It made you believe your body is all there is of you here, in this world. *"Which world?"* you may ask. I hope you do! Because the System is right: in its artificial, virtual, blinding, enslaving, fake world you are nothing but flesh and bones. But in the *real* world you are infinitely more than that – *not a mortal human, but an* ***immortal universal being!***

Look, it's just logical. As human beings, we need spacesuits to work in space or on other planets. As universal beings, we are using a similar sort of "earth suits" to experience a journey called "life" on the planet Earth. Our bodies are such "earth suits."

As any example, this comparison is rough and limited, but it still shows the distance between recognizing the false (waking up) and becoming aware of what's true. What's true is that there is no more difference between you and the world around you than between a single drop of water in the ocean and the ocean itself as a whole.

An even better example would be a hologram. Most of you know what it is. No matter how many parts a holographic picture is broken into, even the smallest part of it will still contain the whole picture down to the smallest detail. It's as if every page of every book in every library in the world contained all the pages of all the books of all libraries.

What does it all have to do with the System, the Illuminati, the New World Order, wars, politics and – *you*? Absolutely everything. Not only such a holographic vision of the universe allows to see what is called "the Big Picture" – it allows to recognize this Big Picture in every smallest "dot" of it, however insignificant and separate from other "dots" it might seem, and to see your reflection in it.

When talking about holograms, we usually imagine them as static pictures, kind of three-dimensional photographs. But in our case, in the case of the universe and ourselves, we are dealing with a dynamic, ever-changing, multi-dimensional hologram where every part not only affects, but literally *creates* the whole.

We have already got used to hear and read that the world belongs to the governments, bankers, United Nations, etc. But no, it does *not*! The world doesn't belong to any group or groups of persons. It belongs to individuals, to each and every one of us. More than that, all those Bliderbergers, Trilateralists, etc., don't really do much, if anything, themselves. They are making plans and decisions, giving out instructions and orders, but it's not them who turn those plans and decisions into actions – it is us, *me* and *you*! We often call them "destructive forces," so it's just logical that it's me, and it's you, who are the only *creative forces* of the world we are living in!

How did it happen that we, Homo *sapiens* ***sapiens***, have so easily, and even happily, bought into the suicidal idea of *living thoughtlessly*?

I repeat, the Illuminati, or whatever you call them, in fact, don't do much, if anything, themselves – they are planning and makeing *us* execute what they've planned. And we readily obey. Look, they don't even force us! Today, the members of the Council on Foreign Relations, the Bilderberg Group, the Trilateral Commission, etc., overtly occupy the key positions of power in the United States and the European Union, ride the United Nations like a bike – where they like. They don't even hide anymore!

Is it because those tiny criminal groups are really so strong, or because we are so weak? To me, in a sense, it's the both: they made us *believe* that we are weak and that they are strong. But in reality, it's the opposite: without us, unwittingly doing their job for them, they would fall down from their heights in a single day! Blind as we are and unwilling to see that when we are trying to fight "the System," we are fighting our own creature; we are fighting *ourselves* as its actual creators.

The solution to this problem is in realizing that we are "mortal humans" only in this *virtual*, "material" world, only in the footnote insidiously added by our self-proclamed "masters" to the endless book of our evolution. Only our bodies are mortal, just as are our T-shirts and jeans – sooner or later they wear out and we throw them away. But we are not our bodies, just as we are not our jeans. We are, always were and will always be, above all, our *individual Souls* – indestructible, all-knowing, and all-creating. We've just been manipulated to forget it.

Have you heard such names as Aurobindo, The Mother (Mirra Alfassa), Satprem, Ghis (formerly Ghislaine Lanctôt)? These people haven't been and are not new "messiahs" or "teachers" of some exotic theories; they have not been, are not, and have nothing to do with those self-proclaimed "guides" that invite you to follow them they themselves don't know where. The people I've named are not only explaining the way they see the world and themselves in it – they were and are ***living so***, giving in practice, in everyday life, the examples of individual freedom (is there other freedom, anyway?), and it's all up to you to decide if you take these examples, and use in your own life, or just leave and forget about them.

Contrary to the "teachings" of the New Age spiritual marketers, *personocratic* vision of the universe and of ourselves, as well as *personocratic* way of thinking and living (read all about it at *www.personocratia.com*), do not require that you get rid of your ego for the benefit of your Soul. Without our egos, we would not survive in the "material" world.

It is quite a different question, however, who – our egos or our Souls – are in control of our thoughts, intentions and acts. For the most of us, it is the ego, whose orders are always loud and clear (mostly mistakenly clear), while the Soul is something we rarely trust because of her barely audible and incomprehensible talk.

We use to say, "*This man (woman) has a Soul,*" or, "*He (she) has no Soul!*" We honestly believe that Soul is a kind of supernatural organ of our body, or a property of our mind. Meanwhile, in reality (and it's the multi-dimensional reality that I'm talking about), it's the opposite: it is our Soul that owns our body, or more precisely, our bodies – physical, astral, mental and emotional, all four belonging to the "material" world and making no sense outside of it. It would thus be just natural if the ego, little and limited as it is, was controlled by the immortal and almighty Soul, and not vice versa. I repeat, there's no question of getting rid of the ego; it's rather like (sorry for such a dubious comparison) giving full *legislative power* inside us to the Soul, while leaving to the ego and mind only the *executive* functions.

I do really and sincerely consider it a solution to the conflicts between us, individuals, and the world we are living in, because one beautiful morning, in August 2008, I woke up with the decision made while I was sleeping: in any situation, no matter what are the circumstances, whatever may happen to me – ***I give carte blanche to my Soul*** in everything that is my life. My mind, my skills, all that I've learned by experience would still stay with me, but, starting from now, on the service of the eternal and almighty part of me, of the universe in me – Her Majesty my Soul (instead of my ego – so strong in fighting the windmills and so weak in facing the real problems).

That's how I'm living ever since. This decision has literally, and dramatically, changed my life, down to every little thing. First of all, I have got rid of the "mother of all fears" – the fear of death. It suddenly became evident to me that this fear is ridiculous and childish: what we call death is not a "dead end" but a doorstep – when the door opens, we simply pass from one room to another, or, even better, come out to a wonderful, limitless, wide open space we had no idea about, but where we all really belong – our true home. The only seeming inconvenience here is that we cannot step back; but seeing the world as it is today and the direction it is being pushed in, would we really want to?

I didn't learn any special technique; tried but never succeeded to attain what is called "meditative state," necessary, people say, to communicate with one's own Soul. Mine continues to "talk" to me in the same barely audible and incomprehensible manner. But it doesn't matter! Her messages arrive to my conscious in the form of intuition, ideas, and projects that move me so much that I cannot help but invest myself into them immediately, entirely and without listening to my ever-complaining mind.

(The mind is always complaining – its domain is logic, reasoning, tactics, and we force it to deal with strategic tasks for which it is not hardwired!)

That was exactly the case of the *Dot Connector* magazine project. In November 2008, I had the idea to start a full-featured, professional, printed bi-monthly. (I worked 30 years in the press, so it was not a problem to make it professional.) The idea didn't come alone but with a clear plan of how to proceed in my very particular situation: I didn't have a cent to invest. It was, by that time, two years that I had lost my last job; as for savings or real estate property, I have never had any of them in my life. But I trusted so much in this project that without hesitation I had dived into debts to make this "impossible" dream come true. It goes without saying that I couldn't pay anybody to assist me and had to do all the jobs myself. (At the very beginning, two friends were honestly willing to help, but left before the release of the very first printed issue. That was not their fault – the project just didn't move them much enough, which only meant that their Souls had for them other plans.) And look, at the time of this writing, the magazine has entered its second year; the 8th issue has just come out! The *Dot Connector* now has subscribers in 14 countries and readers in 51.

When the fear of death goes away, one by one all the other fears follow. This is when, not before, *everything becomes possible* and *nothing impossible*!

It's about the same with the book that you hold in your hands. My ego/mind told me not to even dream about another "impossible" publishing project, but my Soul said, *"Go, go, go!"* And here it is, this book, an "all-material" proof of who to listen to and who to trust – the mind or the Soul.

There were lots of significant synchronicities (some would call them "coincidences") during this year-and-a-half that my Soul has been reigning over everything in my life. Just a week after a hard surgery that I had in the end of December 2009, she unexpectedly made me feel better for a couple of weeks, exactly the time that I needed to finish, print and post to subscribers the 7th issue of the magazine. Omitting the five weeks of "recovery hell" that followed, she again literally brought me back to life (definitely this time, I hope) by the last week of February 2010, so I could "start and finish" the 8th issue. And, last but not least, she has contacted her sisters – the Souls of my friends, known and unknown to me, but all known to her – and together they had collected the amount I missed to print and post the magazine to subscribers. And it's not the first time that she did such a thing.

All this is to say that no matter how loud you cry, "*United we stand!*" – if you are governed by your ego and mind, you may be OK for a while, while the things go more or less well for you; but your mind and ego do not control the world around you, so when the things "suddenly" go worse, you immediately realize that you are alone in the crowd and can count only on your own self, represented, in your case, by the same ego and mind that brought you into this critical situation. (True friends and your family will, of course, be there to help you, but they also risk to make you suffer even harder from your own helplessness.)

It's quite different when you are governed by your Soul – the all-knowing and all-creating part of the universal hologram. As I wrote above, every part of this dynamic hologram at any moment has the power to make changes in the giant hologram of the entire universe. Just imagine what a force it is! And all this incredible force is there to serve *you*! Because the part of the hologram we are talking about is nothing else but *your* Soul – in fact, *it is what you are*! So be sure that she'll make all necessary changes and rearrange, if needed, the whole universe to improve your life the most unexpected way, solve your "insoluble" problems, and do, *just for you*, the things that your ego and mind would consider "impossible."

This is exactly what Gandhi meant when he said, "*Be the change* ***you*** *want to see in the world.*" And this is exactly what John Lennon meant by his ever-actual call, "*War is over, if* ***you*** *want it.*" In both cases, "you" means *you personally*! And in both cases it calls to an individual action *inside* (not outside) of *you*. It is there that the hologram of the world and the universe is created, not in Washington, D.C., not in the City of London, Davos or Brussels. The latter are meeting places of the *impostors* whose power upon you is no more real than they have manipulated you to believe it is. In reality, the only real, creative, unlimited power in the universe is that of *your Soul*, and of your Soul only. Provided, of course, that you consciously, definitely, once and forever liberate her from the authority of your ego and mind. Ego and mind are necessary, good and useful when they are governed by the Soul, but they inevitably become malefic and destructive when they have too much power upon you. They are tools, nothing more. This is their only purpose, their *raison d'être*. Imagine yourself building a house with not you but a hammer controlling the works, and you'll get the picture.

Bear this in mind when reading this book. The selection of articles in it may at first sight seem eclectic, but it's not. The content of the book, as well as of every issue of the *Dot Connector* magazine, is decided by the only authority I unconditionally obey – my Soul, and she always makes sure that under the same cover the reader finds both the problems and the solutions. There are infinitely more problems than solutions, which is quite natural for a very simple reason: it's the couple of ego and mind that creates problems, and the overwhelming majority of people in the so-called civilized world are 100 percent ego/mind driven. As for solutions, and I'm talking about the efficient, really working solutions that only Soul can create, they are as few as the number of people who have abandoned the fears of surviving as "citizens" (i.e., slaves of the System) in favor of living as free human beings, guided by their Souls.

Problems may exist outside of us and can be (and most often are) created by the groups of persons, but real solutions are always inside, always individual, always *yours* and nobody else's. Two persons never see the same things exactly the same way. If one finds a solution to a problem, it doesn't necessarily solve the same problem for you, leaving alone more than a common case when what is a problem for you is not a problem at all for somebody else. This is why thousands of decent people who are ready to act and, if needed, to fight "all together now" for truth and freedom, but fully governed by their egos and minds, are condemned to endlessly fight the windmills. *There is nothing outside but the windmills!*

There are no solutions "for all," only for ***every one***. Nobody in the world knows better than I what is good for me. So nobody can replace me in finding, or, more precisely, *creating* solutions that suit me best. I'm far from being the first to create my own universal solution to all the problems I'm facing or may face in the future – this solution, for me, is *giving carte blanche to my Soul* by transferring to her all the power upon myself as a part of the hologram of the universe, and by taking away this power from my ego and mind. (The latter have resisted – and actively! – for almost a year, but finally accepted the new status quo.)

So, I have made my choice, my *last* choice. "Last," because my Soul, just as anyone else's, knows everything – the past, the "here and now," and the future. At any given moment, she knows what is best, what is true, and doesn't need to make choices. Long before I was born on this planet, she had already chosen for me the path. The rule of the game, however, is that I am not supposed to know it. While, like the most of us, I was governed by my ego and listened to the reasoning of my mind, my life resembled the endless and futile attempts to win in a casino. Now it's as though I became the casino owner ("the house always wins!") – and it seems like my Soul has appreciated that I finally gave her the role she deserves by her very nature.

No, she didn't make my life "better" financially. She has just changed me so that I simply don't care about "things" anymore.

I'm no more "surviving" – I'm *living*. I feel myself free as never before. And freedom, first of and above all, is freedom from those thousands of little fears that are living inside all of us and which we usually aren't even aware of. Of course, I still haven't got rid of them all – they resist and obstinately try to get back. But I know, and I feel, that they are much weaker now, in the absence of their "dear mom" – the fear of death.

Taken too seriously, life is unbearable; to make it fun, take it funny! The worst thing that may happen to me is that I will cross the doorstep and find myself in ... a much better place!

Of course, I am joking ... and not. What I know for sure from my Soul is that the journey through life on the planet Earth she had planned for me is far from being over. Too many things left to do, and the most important of them is making evident to as many persons as possible, in the *Dot Connector* and in books like this one, that whatever the problem is –

***you** are the solution!*

"Nothing in this world works the way you think it does.
Nothing.
The police aren't who you think they are;
the sheriff is not who you think he is;
banks do not do what you think they do;
governments don't operate anywhere near the way
you think they do.
And that's why today, when you look at what's going on
in the world, none of it makes any sense. It's all crazy.
It makes no sense at all."

Jordan Maxwell,
at the Project Camelot "Awake and Aware" Conference,
Los Angeles, September 20, 2009.

"A slave is one who waits for someone to come and free him."

Ezra Pound,
American poet (1885-1972).

Climategate: A Crime Against Humanity

Michael Rivero

Politicians seek to gain wealth and power and authority by taking something that occurs naturally, transforming it and promoting it as a crisis, and then selling the population a solution in exchange for higher taxes and increased authority over their lives.

Climategate: The Mother of All Deceptions

"The whole aim of practical politics is to keep the populace alarmed (and hence clamorous to be led to safety) by menacing it with an endless series of hobgoblins, all of them imaginary." – H. L. Mencken.

"Our job is to give people not what they want, but what we decide they ought to have." – Richard Salent, Former President CBS News.

The recent exposures of fraud coming from the Hadley Climate Research Unit, then followed by similar exposures at New Zealand's NWIA, Australia's climate center, and NOAA,[1] have only confirmed the doubts arising from the obviously non-scientific methods employed by the anthropogenic global warming supporters, hereinafter called the "Global Warming Cult." I call them a cult because of the abandonment of scientific method by many of the acolytes, together with a recent British Court decision that declared belief in global warming was accorded the status of a religion.[2]

Human-caused global warming is not being researched, it is being *promoted*. Al Gore and his fellow investors have spent over a hundred million dollars in creating a crisis of human-caused global warming out of (quite literally) thin air. They are not doing this out of the goodness of their hearts. They expect to reap billions in profits from the trading of carbon credits, a "license to pollute" available for a price and subject to brokerage fees. One of the people Al Gore relied on to create this scheme was Ken Lay, late of Enron, aka the Crooked "E." Al Gore plans to use carbon dioxide to do to the world what Ken Lay did to California using electricity – loot the people!

Coincident with the desire to reap huge profits from the general population of the world is the agenda to promote a global government. Currently, the push for a global government rests on three pillars. Global warming is one of them. The other two pillars exploited to create the "need" for a global government are a global Swine Flu pandemic, requiring a global health organization, and a global financial crisis, requiring a global bank. The political power behind this push for global government is immense – enough to win Al Gore an Academy Award and a Nobel Peace Prize for his film, *An Inconvenient Truth*, despite a court ruling pointing out the numerous provable lies and distortions in it.[3]

To any real objective observer, the methods employed by the Cult are not those of science and research but of salesmanship and propaganda. Scare tactics are well in evidence. To anyone of an age enough to recall previous scare campaigns, the hue and cry for anthropogenic global warming is reminiscent of "killer bees" and Y2K scares of yesteryear.

To put it bluntly, anthropogenic global warming is a load of government-sponsored bovine excrement. Its purpose is to trick you out of money and into obedience. And despite the shrill cries of those who insist that government would never conceive or let along execute such a monstrous fraud upon the people, the fact is that anthropogenic global warming has a very long pedigree of deception behind it.

Here are some examples.

Ancient Lies

Ramses and the Hittites

In Egypt, one of the greatest surviving monuments (and source of tourism revenues) is the great temple at Abu Simbel. Built by Ramses II, known as Ramses the Great (by his own admission), the walls at Abu

Simbel are carved with a unique style called "sunken relief," a method of artwork that was less expensive than full bas relief and more difficult to erase. And there, depicted in indelible sunken relief cross the walls and pylons of Abu Simbel, are scenes of Ramses the Great, victorious in battle against the Hittites at the battle of Kadesh. Immortalized in stone is his victory for all to see. Similar carvings at Abydos and Luxor also show Ramses defeating the Hittites at Kadesh.

Except... Ramses the Great did *not* defeat anyone at Kadesh. Fed false information by Hittite spies, Ramses led his men into a trap and barely avoided losing his entire army. Ramses was forced to sign a peace treaty with the Hittites (the first non-aggression treaty in history), ending Egypt's expansion into the north.

Ramses, like any head of state, had a huge ego and together with not wishing to appear less than godlike to his population (who were taught that he was a God), Ramses promoted the idea that the battle in Kadesh had been a great victory for Egypt, certain that most Egyptians lacked the means to actually travel to Kadesh and find out for themselves what the truth was. (The Canaanites did find out and, emboldened by Ramses' lack of victory, revolted, thereby ending Egypt's dominion beyond the Sinai.)

There is a motto here. Rulers serve bovine excrement to their own people in order to control them. That is a fact carved in stone for all to see, 3200 years ago. It is no less true today than it was in the time of the pharaohs.

The Donation of Constantine

Prior to the time of Constantine, kingship was either won in battle or inherited from father to son. There was no specific ceremony upon taking the throne (although one finds records of some very wild parties held in celebration). But in the time of Constantine, the church invented for itself the ritual of coronation, in which the Bishop of Rome prayed over Constantine and then slapped a crown on his head, thereby sending out a clear message that the church claimed responsibility for Constantine's earthly power and authority.

Following Constantine's death, a document appeared, in which Constantine purportedly donated the imperial regalia of Rome to the Church, with the request that it be "loaned" to all future rulers of the Roman Empire. From that day on, the loan took the form of the ritual of coronation, in which the holy oil of anointment created the king, rather than conquest or the bloodline. Coronation added the imprimatur of God's will to the legitimacy of the monarch, and as an inevitable corollary, nobody could ascend to the throne without the permission and blessing of the Church.

Except... Constantine had not been informed ahead of time of his own coronation and by all accounts was rather shocked and angered by the Church's brazen attempt to portray his civil authority as a gift of their religion. As for the "donation of Constantine," which literally reshaped the political history of Europe for half a millennium, it was a forgery, most likely written within the Papal offices, to steal for the Church the right to declare who would or would not be kings of Europe.

There is a motto here. Bovine excrement is shoveled out of places besides the civil government.

Prester John

In the 1130s, the Turkish Empire under the leadership of Imad ad-din Zengi began to encroach on the Crusader Kingdoms of the Holy Land. Most Crusaders considered their vows to the first Holy Crusade fulfilled and had already returned to Europe, leaving the Pilgrim road from Jaffa to Jerusalem under the guard of the newly emergent Knights Templar (who seemed to spend all their time digging under the Temple Mount). The Knights Templar, although able to guard a road when not shoveling dirt, were insufficient a force to hold off an entire invasion, and in 1145, Hugh, Bishop of Jabala, was sent to meet the newly enthroned Pope Blessed Eugene III to ask for help. Pope Eugene, far less bloodthirsty than his predecessors, balked at a new and costly crusade so soon after the previous one. Hugh told the Pope that a new crusade to preserve Christian dominion over the Holy Lands would be easy and cheap, because somewhere far to the east of the Holy Lands was the Kingdom of Prester John.

Prester (or Presbyter) John was a Christian king, a direct descendant of one of the Magi who had visited the infant Jesus and reportedly whose kingdom was powerful, wealthy, and peaceful. According to Hugh, Prester John was committed to preserving Christian rule over the Holy Lands, and awaited only a sign of equal commitment from the armies of Europe. Rumors of the impending intervention of Prester John bolstered the courage of the Christians of the Crusader Kingdoms and of Europe, and based in part on the promise of Prester John as an ally, Pope Eugene launched the Second Holy Crusade, led by Louis VII of France and Conrad III of Germany. But Prester John did not show up as promised. The Second Crusade ended in the route of the Crusader armies at Damascus, and the Christians found themselves holding less of the Holy Lands.

In 1165, just as the situation in the Holy Lands began to deteriorate further, a letter began to circulate around Europe, purportedly from Prester John. The letter again promised support for the Christian armies of Europe. The letter included descriptions of the wonders of Prester John's kingdom. The letter was so popular it was copied far and wide, and portions of it set to music!

But again, Prester John did not show up when promised, and in 1187 Jerusalem fell to Saladin. This prompted the start of the Third Crusade. Once again, rumors of Prester John's armies attacking the Muslims from the East bolstered the invading forces.

Except... Prester John was the invention of the Church, a propaganda device to trick Europeans to join a war, in which they were clearly outnumbered by the opposing force. As Marco Polo and other travelers brought tales of the Orient back to Europe in the 13th century, Church leaders grew alarmed as Christians learned of powerful and advanced civilizations to the east that existed without any awareness of Christianity. Following a brief period when the Dominicans unsuccessfully denounced Marco Polo's writings as heresy and fraud, the Church again revived the legends of Prester John to prove that Christianity did rule in the far east. Highly fanciful maps were produced of just where Prester John's kingdom would be found.

The legends of Prester John persisted from the 12th to the 17th centuries even though John himself could not have lived that long. Numerous expeditions to find the Kingdom of Prester John were mounted, all without success. As the map of Asia became filled in accurately with no sign of the fabled Christian kingdom, the legend was altered to claim that Prester John's Kingdom was actually in Ethiopia, then, as the African map started to fill in, further south in "Darkest Africa." The realm of Prester John eventually became one of the fabled "Lost Kingdoms of Africa " that lured explorers into the Congo, often to their deaths.

As for the letter purportedly from Prester John, like the Donation of Constantine, it was a clever forgery. In its original version it was apparently derived mostly from Otto von Freisingen's historical account of the story told by Hugh, Bishop of Jabala to Pope Eugene. The story of Prester

John's palace was actually a description of the palace of St. Thomas the Apostle. As the letter was recopied through the centuries, the stories it contained grew ever more fanciful, filled with strange and wonderful creatures and amazing feats of magic and science. In the 18th century these stories of the land of Prester John were revived as part of the tales of Baron Munchausen. In 1988, the stories of the land of Prester John again surfaced in Terry Gilliam's film, *The Adventures of Baron Munchausen.*

The motto here is: A really big lie can last a long time, and there may even be a movie deal in it!

The Seven Cities of Gold

In the year 711, General Tarik ibn Ziyad led his forces across from Africa to Iberia, and commencing with "Tarik's Mountain" (Gibraltar) conquered all of Spain in mere months. As would be the case with the Templars, following their arrest and execution by Philip Le Belle, stories abounded of the treasures of the Spanish churches smuggled away from the invading armies by seven bishops and hidden from view.

Then, following Columbus' discovery of the New World, and perhaps in the realization that whatever it was Columbus had discovered on the far side of the Atlantic was not the Indies he had originally promised, a new story began to surface that the Seven Bishops who had fled Spain in 711 had somehow made their way to the New World and used their treasure to found seven Christian cities. Like the Kingdom of Prester John, these were rumored to be cities of immense wealth.

The lure of these mythical cities aided the Spanish explorers in recruiting men for the dangerous business of sailing the Atlantic followed by conquest of an unknown land. A shipwrecked sailor, Cabeza de Vaca, claimed to have seen cities decorated with huge gems. Following Vaca's descriptions, Fray Marcos de Niza in 1539 claimed to have seen cities with tall gold buildings. It is possible that Niza actually saw adobe buildings shining with silica and pyrite in the sunlight from a distance, but following the killing of his servant avoided close approach to the indigenous people. Despite the absence of provenance, the stories of the Seven Cities of Gold drew both Cortez and Coronado deeper into the New World. The natives quickly realized the lethality of denying the existence of the cities of gold, and simply pointed the Spaniards further inland, promising that the cities were just over the next mountain range.

Except... There were no cities of gold. They were a propaganda device used to motivate the explorers' crews in the conquest of the New World, and while they did find gold, the real result of the tale of the Seven Cities of Gold was that Spain pushed all the way into what is now California and New Mexico.

The motto here is that even with gold plating, bovine excrement remains bovine excrement.

The Witches

In the year 1200, Europe entered a period of prolonged cooling, which lasted until the mid 1800s. This is called the "Little Ice Age." Europeans did not understand climate and, owing to theocratic rule following the collapse of Rome, had turned their backs on science. All that happened was presumed the will of God. Priests prayed to God to halt the glaciers advancing on the villages. But as the villages succumbed to the ice, the Church, rather than admit to failure, began to blame supernatural magical forces for the increasing cold. Seeking a scapegoat, the Church set upon those individuals who still held knowledge outside that allowed by the churches. These educated and wise people, people with "wit", were declared heretics and "witches." A phrase in the Bible, "Thou shalt not suffer a poisoner to live" was re-translated into "Thou shalt not suffer a *witch* to live", and the Church now had the perfect scapegoat to blame the unstoppable cold on.

For the next three centuries, up until the incident at Salem, Massachusetts, innocent people were blamed by the Church for everything that went wrong. If something bad happened that God could not make go away, it was because of the witches. Cold weather? Blame the witches. Plagues? Blame the witches. Failed crops and livestock? Blame the witches. Witch-hunting became a full time profession. The accusers and prosecutors grew rich on the confiscated wealth of the condemned. Politicians, business competitors, and even jealous wives quickly learned that they could dispose of a rival with impunity with a simple accusation of witchcraft.

Except... There are no witches as conceptualized by the Church. No witches able to hop on a broomstick and interfere with passenger jets. No witch was ever able to transform himself or herself into an animal. It is all make-believe, and it makes for great books and fun movies, but the evil crimes depicted in the *Maleus Malificarum* never occurred. The confessions, on which the church assurances of witchcraft were based, were extracted under torture, some forms of which are sadly still in use in the United States today. Yes, there are people who like to call themselves witches, but their craft at most is limited to natural medicines and midwifery.

For three centuries religiously induced terror and horror stalked across the landscape in Europe. As the grains and cereals, on which Europe had fed, failed, much hardier potatoes were introduced. But the Church declared them the food of the devil, because they grew in the ground. Millions starved standing on an abundant food supply, afraid that eating the potato would condemn their souls to hell. When the plagues hit Europe, religious flagellants traveled from town to town, spreading the disease in the droplets of blood flung from the ends of their whips. As the epidemic accelerated in the wake of such rituals, the Church fanned the blood-lust for the witches.

Nobody really knows how many people were tortured and killed during the witch trials. The numbers increase and decrease depending on the agenda of who is reporting the numbers. Conservative estimates of victims executed for being witches is a quarter of a million. Estimates of those tortured and then released are considerably higher.

Of all the madness and self-delusions man has collectively engaged in, the search for and execution of witches stands as a monument to all that is dark and fearful in the human mind. A few grew rich and powerful while around them a million people writhed in agony and death. If there is a moral to be found here, it is that the execution of accused witches in Mexico in the 1990s (and the evils of Guantánamo Bay) proves that we are not as far from the rack and the stake as we would like to pretend. We comfort ourselves with the idea that the dark ages are long ago and far removed from our modern enlightened age, but the truth is that fanatics can tear down civilization rather quickly. You burn the Library at Alexandria, flay the librarian alive, burn the rest of the books to heat the public baths and set fire to anyone who refuses to bow to the bovine excrement.

More Recent Deceptions

President McKinley told the American people that the USS *Maine* had been sunk in Havana Harbor by a Spanish mine. The American people, outraged by this apparent unprovoked attack, supported the Spanish-American War. The Captain of the USS *Maine* had insisted the ship was sunk by a coal bin explosion; investigations after the war proved that such had indeed been the case. There had been no mine.

Hitler used this principle of lying to his own people to initiate an invasion. He told the people of Germany that Poland had attacked first, and staged fake attacks against German targets. The Germans, convinced they were being threatened, followed Hitler into Poland and into World War II.

FDR claimed Pearl Harbor was a surprise attack. *It wasn't.*[4] The United States saw war with Japan as the means to get into war with Germany, which Americans opposed. So Roosevelt needed Japan to appear to strike first. Following an 8-step plan devised by the Office of Naval Intelligence,[5] Roosevelt intentionally provoked Japan into the attack. Contrary to the official story, the Japanese fleet did not maintain radio silence, but sent messages intercepted and decoded by US intercept stations.[6] Tricked by the lie of a surprise attack, Americans marched off to war.

President Johnson lied about the Gulf of Tonkin[7] to send Americans off to fight in Vietnam. There were no torpedoes in the water in the Gulf. LBJ took advantage of an inexperienced sonar man's erroneous report of an attack to goad Congress into escalating the Vietnam War.

Then there were the lies used to trick the US into war with Iraq.

First off was Tony Blair's "Dodgy Dossier,"[8] a document released by the Prime Minister that made many of the claims used to support the push for war. The dossier soon collapsed when it was revealed that much of it had been plagiarized from a student thesis paper that was 12 years old! The contents of the dossier, however much they seemed to create a good case for invasion, were obsolete and outdated.

Then there was the claim about the "mobile biological weapons laboratories." Proffered in the absence of any real laboratories in the wake of the invasion, photos of these trailers were shown on all the US mainstream

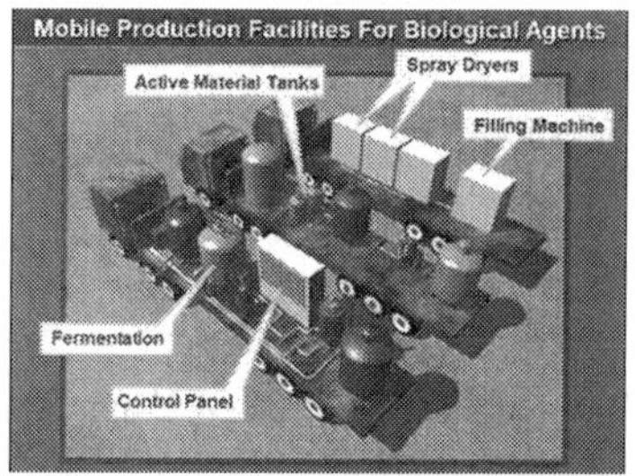

media with the claim that, while seeming to lack anything suggesting biological processing, these were parts of a much larger assembly of multiple trailers that churned out biological weapons of mass destruction.

The chief proponent of this hoax was Colin Powell, who presented these illustrations to the United Nations on February 5th, 2003.[9] This claim fell apart when it was revealed that the trailers were nothing more than hydrogen gas generators used to inflate weather balloons. This fact was already known to both the US and UK, as a British company manufactured the units and sold them to Iraq.

Colin Powell's speech to the UN was itself one misstatement after another. Powell claimed that Iraq had purchased special aluminum tubes whose only possible use was in uranium enrichment centrifuges. Both CIA and Powell's own State Department confirmed that the tubes were parts for missiles Saddam was legally allowed to have. Following the invasion, no centrifuges, aluminum or otherwise were found.

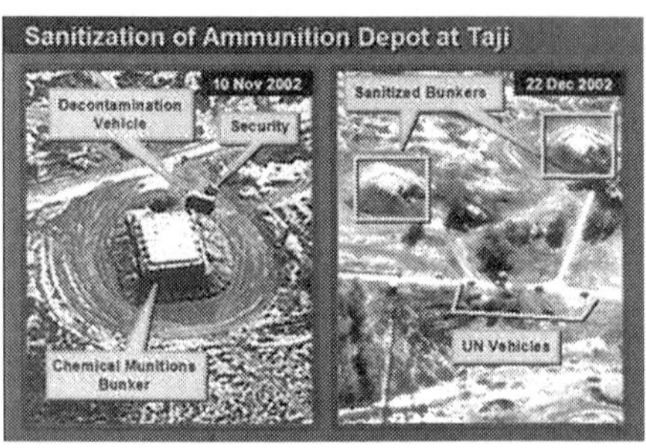

Powell also claimed to the United Nations that the photo on the left showed "decontamination vehicles". But when United Nations inspectors visited the site after the invasion, they located the vehicles and discovered they were just fire-fighting equipment.

Powell claimed the Iraqis had illegal rockets and launchers hidden in the palm trees of Western Iraq. None was ever found. Powell claimed that the Iraqis had 8,500 liters (2,245 gallons) of anthrax. None was ever found.

Powell claimed that Iraq had four tons of VX nerve gas. The UN had already confirmed that it was destroyed. The only VX ever found were samples the US had left as "standards" for testing. When the UN suspected that the US samples had been used to contaminate Iraqi warheads, the US moved quickly to destroy the samples before comparison tests could be carried out.[10]

Powell claimed that Iraq was building long-range remote drones specifically designed to carry biological weapons. The only drones found were short-range reconnaissance drones.

Powell claimed that Iraq had an aggregate of between 100 and 500 tons of chemical and biological warfare agents. Powell gave no basis for that claim at all, and a DIA report issued the same time directly contradicted the claim. No biological or chemical weapons were found in Iraq following the invasion. Powell claimed that "unnamed sources" confirmed that Saddam had authorized his field commanders to use biological weapons. No such weapons were ever used by the Iraqis to defend against the invasion and, of course, none were ever found in Iraq.

Powell claimed that 122 mm warheads found by the UN inspectors were chemical weapons. The warheads were empty, and showed no signs of ever having contained chemical weapons. Powell claimed that Iraq had a secret force of illegal long-range Scud missiles. None were ever found.

Powell claimed to have an audio tape proving that Saddam was supporting Osama Bin Laden. But independent translation of the tape revealed Osama's wish for Saddam's death.[11]

Colin Powell's UN debacle also included spy photos taken from high flying aircraft and spacecraft. On the photos were circles and arrows and labels pointing to various fuzzy white blobs and identifying them as laboratories and storage areas for Saddam's massive weapons of mass destruction program. Nothing in the photos actually suggested what the blobby shapes were, and during inspections, which followed the invasion, all of them turned out to be rather benign.

In at least one case, the satellite Powell claimed had taken one of the pictures had actually been *out of operation* at the time.[12] And many questioned why Powell was showing black and white photos when the satellites in use at the time over Iraq took color images.[13]

Another piece of evidence consists of documents, which President Bush referenced to in his 2003 State of the Union speech. According to Bush, these documents proved that Iraq was buying tons of uranium oxide, called "Yellow Cake," from Niger. Since Israel had bombed Iraq's nuclear power plant years before, it was claimed that the only reason Saddam would have for buying uranium oxide was to build bombs. This hoax fell apart fast when it was pointed out that Iraq has a great deal of uranium ore inside their own borders and no need to import any from Niger or anywhere else. The IAEA then blew the cover off the fraud by announcing that the documents Bush had used were not only forgeries,[14] but too obvious to believe that anyone in the Bush administration did not know they were forgeries! The forged documents were reported as being "discovered" in Italy by SISMI, the Italian security service. Shortly before the "discovery" the head of SISMI had been paid a visit by Michael Ledeen, Manucher Ghorbanifar, and two officials from OSP, one of whom was Larry Franklin, the Israeli spy operating inside the OSP. In July 2005, the Italian Parliament concluded their own investigation and named four men as suspects in the creation of the forged documents: Michael Ledeen, Dewey Clarridge, Ahmed Chalabi and Francis Brookes. This report has been included in Patrick Fitzgerald's investigation into the outing of Valerie Plame and Paul McNulty, the prosecutor of the AIPAC spy case.

A recently declassified memo proves that the State Department reported the fact that the Niger documents were forgeries to the CIA *11 days before* President Bush made the claim about the Niger uranium based on those documents.

In the end, the real proof that we were lied to about Iraq's WMD is that no WMD were ever found. That means that every single piece of paper that purported to prove that Iraq had weapons of mass destruction was by default a fraud, a hoax, and a lie. There could be no evidence that supported the claim that Iraq had weapons of mass destruction, because Iraq did not have weapons of mass destruction. In a way, the existence of any faked documents about Iraq's WMD is actually an admission of guilt. If one is taking the time to create fake documents, the implication is that the faker is already aware that there are no genuine documents.

All that the US Government had were copied student papers, forged documents, balloon inflators posing as portable bioweapons labs, and photos with misleading labels on them.

The President of the United States and his neocon associates lied to the people of the United States to send them off on a war of conquest.

Scaring the Public for Fun and Profit

"News is what someone wants to suppress. Everything else is advertising."

– Richard Salent, Former President CBS News.

Manufactured rumors of imminent doom have been around as long as religion itself.[15] Predictions that the world is about to come to an end appear at regular intervals throughout the history of humankind, usually followed by demands of money and obedience to avert disaster, or guarantee salvation. But in the modern age, where fewer and fewer people are blindly religious, doomsayers have had to eschew the trappings of the religious prophet and don the garb of the scientific prognosticator. However, their track record of success in predicting the end of the world had fared no better than that of their clerical brethren!

The Killer Bees

One of the fastest ways to get attention and funding is to announce the imminent doom of the world, then ask for money and/or obedience to study and perhaps "solve" the problem.

In the 1970s, alarmists warned that a deadly strain of African "killer bees," accidentally released in Brazil in 1957, were slowly moving towards the United States. The media was filled with lurid stories of vengeance-minded bees slaughtering innocent humans. Movies and TV were filled with killer bee horror films (or comedic skits such as the "Killer Bees" on *Saturday Night Live*).

Starting in 2002, the "killer bees" did in fact arrive in the United States. And contrary to the warnings, they do not attack people at random. Like any other bee, they will act to defend their hives when attacked, but since most Americans are smart enough not to do that with ordinary bees, the prophecies of doom and death never materialized.

As a side note, apiculturists already knew that the "killer bee" alarm was overblown. Worker bees, killer or otherwise, can only sting once, and usually die afterwards. Only the Queen Bees, which never leave the hive after their mating flight, are able to sting multiple times and survive. So bees, killer or otherwise, do not sting unless they are provoked to the point of a Kamikaze suicide attack on the enemy.

Y2K

As the 20th century wound down, concern was raised over the fact that most calendar functions inside computers were "hardwired" with the leading "19," and that as of midnight, December 31, 1999, computer date functions would leap backwards one hundred years to January 1, 1900. The media was filled with dire forecasts of passenger jets falling out of the skies, banks unable to operate, a stock market crash, power grid collapse, etc., etc., etc.

Now, while it was true that some dedicated clock and calendar chips did in fact have the hardwired "19" problem, the reality is that most calendar functions were already being handled totally in software, and for those that were not, a changeover to software calendars able to deal with the year 2000 was a trivial exercise. But so convincing were the scaremongers that the public started pulling their money out of banks in anticipation of a crash. As a result, corporations had to spend far more money on demonstrations to convince the public that Y2K was fixed than they spent fixing Y2K. In the end, Y2K turned into a 6 billion dollar enterprise that reaped huge profits for the scaremongerers-turned-software patch and "assurance testing" entrepreneurs.

Y2K came and went, and none of the doom-and-gloom prophecies came to pass.[16]

Global Warming in 1817

"It will without doubt have come to your Lordship's knowledge that a considerable change of climate, inexplicable at present to us, must have taken place in the Circumpolar Regions, by which the severity of the cold that has for centuries past enclosed the seas in the high northern latitudes in an impenetrable barrier of ice has been during the last two years, greatly abated. [This] affords ample proof that new sources of warmth have been opened and give us leave to hope that the Arctic Seas may at this time be more accessible than they have been for centuries past, and that discoveries may now be made in them not only interesting to the advancement of science but also to the future intercourse of mankind and the commerce of distant nations." – President of the Royal Society, London, to the Admiralty, 20th November, 1817.

The Coming Ice Age (1975)

As strange as it may seem, back in the 1970s, *Newsweek* reported that climatologists were warning that Earth was headed into a new Ice Age (see facsimile on the right). That prophecy didn't work out either.

But all the way back in 1922, global warming was the fashion! (See facsimile on page 16.) And again in 1958, global warming was the fashion![17]

A lesson to be learned from the above is that governments, religious leaders, TV networks, con men of all persuasions are constantly warning you of something you ought to be afraid of, or are possibly the cause of, and in any event are able to avoid/atone for with enough cold hard cash.

SCIENCE

The Cooling World

There are ominous signs that the earth's weather patterns have begun to change dramatically and that these changes may portend a drastic decline in food production—with serious political implications for just about every nation on earth. The drop in food output could begin quite soon, perhaps only ten years from now. The regions destined to feel its impact are the great wheat-producing lands of Canada and the U.S.S.R. in the north, along with a number of marginally self-sufficient tropical areas—parts of India, Pakistan, Bangladesh, Indochina and Indonesia—where the growing season is dependent upon the rains brought by the monsoon.

The evidence in support of these predictions has now begun to accumulate so massively that meteorologists are hard-pressed to keep up with it. In England, farmers have seen their growing season decline by about two weeks since 1950, with a resultant over-all loss in grain production estimated at up to 100,000 tons annually. During the same time, the average temperature around the equator has risen by a fraction of a degree—a fraction that in some areas can mean drought and desolation. Last April, in the most devastating outbreak of tornadoes ever recorded, 148 twisters killed more than 300 people and caused half a billion dollars' worth of damage in thirteen U.S. states.

Trend: To scientists, these seemingly disparate incidents represent the advance signs of fundamental changes in the world's weather. The central fact is that after three quarters of a century of extraordinarily mild conditions, the earth's climate seems to be cooling down. Meteorologists disagree about the cause and extent of the cooling trend, as well as over its specific impact on local weather conditions. But they are almost unanimous in the view that the trend will reduce agricultural productivity for the rest of the century. If the climatic change is as profound as some of the pessimists fear, the resulting famines could be catastrophic. "A major climatic change would force economic and social adjustments on a worldwide scale," warns a recent report by the National Academy of Sciences, "because the global patterns of food production and population that have evolved are implicitly dependent on the climate of the present century."

A survey completed last year by Dr. Murray Mitchell of the National Oceanic and Atmospheric Administration reveals a drop of half a degree in average ground temperatures in the Northern Hemisphere between 1945 and 1968. According to George Kukla of Columbia University, satellite photos indicated a sudden, large increase in Northern Hemisphere snow cover in the winter of 1971-72. And a study released last month by two NOAA scientists notes that the amount of sunshine reaching the ground in the continental U.S. diminished by 1.3 per cent between 1964 and 1972.

To the layman, the relatively small changes in temperature and sunshine can be highly misleading. Reid Bryson of the University of Wisconsin points out that the earth's average temperature during the great Ice Ages was only about 7 degrees lower than during its warmest eras—and that the present decline has taken the planet about a sixth of the way toward the Ice Age average. Others regard the cooling as a reversion to the "little ice age" conditions that brought bitter winters to much of Europe and northern America between 1600 and 1900—years when the Thames used to freeze so solidly that Londoners roasted oxen on the ice and when iceboats sailed the Hudson River almost as far south as New York City.

Just what causes the onset of major and minor ice ages remains a mystery. "Our knowledge of the mechanisms of climatic change is at least as fragmentary as our data," concedes the National Academy of Sciences report. "Not only are the basic scientific questions largely unanswered, but in many cases we do not yet know enough to pose the key questions."

Extremes: Meteorologists think that they can forecast the short-term results of the return to the norm of the last century. They begin by noting the slight drop in over-all temperature that produces large numbers of pressure centers in the upper atmosphere. These break up the smooth flow of westerly winds over temperate areas. The stagnant air produced in this way causes an increase in extremes of local weather such as droughts, floods, extended dry spells, long freezes, delayed monsoons and even local temperature increases—all of which have a direct impact on food supplies.

"The world's food-producing system," warns Dr. James D. McQuigg of NOAA's Center for Climatic and Environmental Assessment, "is much more sensitive to the weather variable than it was even five years ago." Furthermore, the growth of world population and creation of new national boundaries make it impossible for starving peoples to migrate from their devastated fields, as they did during past famines.

Climatologists are pessimistic that political leaders will take any positive action to compensate for the climatic change, or even to allay its effects. They concede that some of the more spectacular solutions proposed, such as melting the arctic ice cap by covering it with black soot or diverting arctic rivers, might create problems far greater than those they solve. But the scientists see few signs that government leaders anywhere are even prepared to take the simple measures of stockpiling food or of introducing the variables of climatic uncertainty into economic projections of future food supplies. The longer the planners delay, the more difficult will they find it to cope with climatic change once the results become grim reality.

—PETER GWYNNE with bureau reports

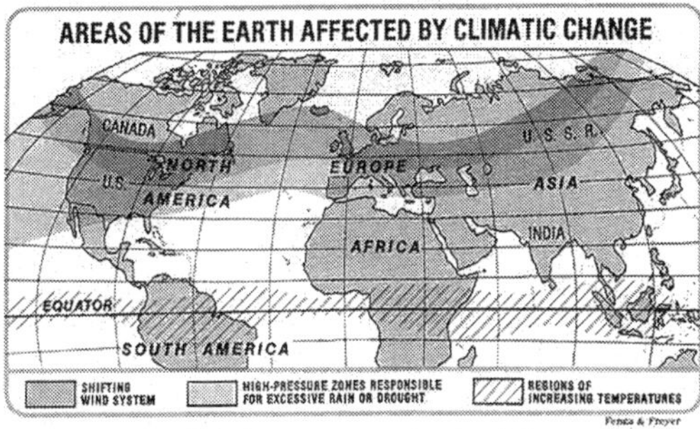

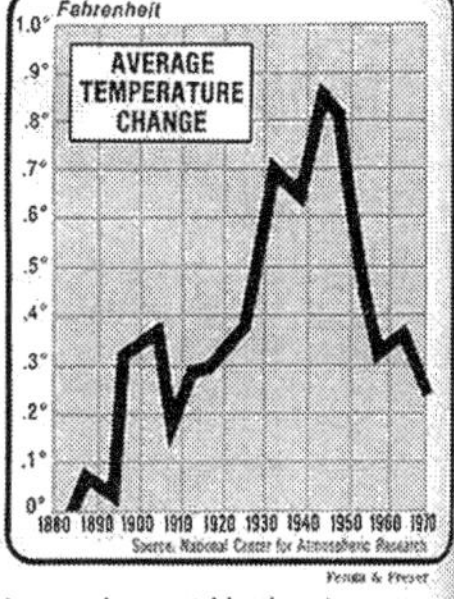

64 Newsweek, April 28, 1975

The article in *Newsweek* (April 28, 1975) predicting the beginning of dramatic global cooling, which *"may portend a drastic decline in food production"* and *"would force economic and social adjustments on a worldwide scale."*

NOVEMBER, 1922. MONTHLY WEATHER REVIEW.

THE CHANGING ARCTIC.

By GEORGE NICOLAS IFFT.

[Under date of October 10, 1922, the American consul at Bergen, Norway, submitted the following report to the State Department, Washington, D. C.]

The Arctic seems to be warming up. Reports from fishermen, seal hunters, and explorers who sail the seas about Spitzbergen and the eastern Arctic, all point to a radical change in climatic conditions, and hitherto unheard-of high temperatures in that part of the earth's surface.

In August, 1922, the Norwegian Department of Commerce sent an expedition to Spitzbergen and Bear Island under the leadership of Dr. Adolf Hoel, lecturer on geology at the University of Christiania. Its purpose was to survey and chart the lands adjacent to the Norwegian mines on those islands, take soundings of the adjacent waters, and make other oceanographic investigations.

Dr. Hoel, who has just returned, reports the location of hitherto unknown coal deposits on the eastern shores of Advent Bay—deposits of vast extent and superior quality. This is regarded as of first importance, as so far most of the coal mined by the Norwegian companies on those islands has not been of the best quality.

R. L. Holmes: Quart. Journ, Royal Meteorol. Soc., January, 1905.

The oceanographic observations have, however, been even more interesting. Ice conditions were exceptional. In fact, so little ice has never before been noted. The expedition all but established a record, sailing as far north as 81° 29′ in ice-free water. This is the farthest north ever reached with modern oceanographic apparatus.

The character of the waters of the great polar basin has heretofore been practically unknown. Dr. Hoel reports that he made a section of the Gulf Stream at 81° north latitude and took soundings to a depth of 3,100 meters. These show the Gulf Stream very warm, and it could be traced as a surface current till beyond the 81st parallel. The warmth of the waters makes it probable that the favorable ice conditions will continue for some time.

Later a section was taken of the Gulf Stream off Bear Island and off the Isfjord, as well as a section of the cold current that comes down along the west coast of Spitzbergen off the south cape.

In connection with Dr. Hoel's report, it is of interest to note the unusually warm summer in Arctic Norway and the observations of Capt. Martin Ingebrigtsen, who has sailed the eastern Arctic for 54 years past. He says that he first noted warmer conditions in 1918, that since that time it has steadily gotten warmer, and that to-day the Arctic of that region is not recognizable as the same region of 1868 to 1917.

Many old landmarks are so changed as to be unrecognizable. Where formerly great masses of ice were found, there are now often moraines, accumulations of earth and stones. At many points where glaciers formerly extended far into the sea they have entirely disappeared.

The change in temperature, says Captain Ingebrigtsen, has also brought about great change in the flora and fauna of the Arctic. This summer he sought for white fish in Spitzbergen waters. Formerly great shoals of them were found there. This year he saw none, although he visited all the old fishing grounds.

There were few seal in Spitzbergen waters this year, the catch being far under the average. This, however, did not surprise the captain. He pointed out that formerly the waters about Spitzbergen held an even summer temperature of about 3° Celsius; this year recorded temperatures up to 15°, and last winter the ocean did not freeze over even on the north coast of Spitzbergen.

With the disappearance of white fish and seal has come other life in these waters. This year herring in great shoals were found along the west coast of Spitzbergen, all the way from the fry to the veritable great herring. Shoals of smelt were also met with.

What is Global Warming?

Let's get something straight: the climate is supposed to change. In four-and-a-half billion years, there has never been a time when the Earth's climate remained exactly the same. Careful study of the geological and paleontological record shows that the climate is always changing, that the Earth is always getting warmer or colder in long hundred thousand year cycles.

At present, the Earth is far colder than the Cretaceous, but far warmer than the ice ages. Given that the Earth has only recently come out of the Little Ice Age, it stands to reason we should be getting warmer. It's the idea that the Earth can be locked into a particular configuration that is unnatural. And who was to decide what the ideal temperature should be? What is ideal for people living at the equator is hardly ideal for those living in the polar regions.

Global warming cultists like to talk about the balance of nature. This is a very romantic term. But there is no balance of nature. Nature is change. Nature is chaos. Nature is one life form going extinct while another evolves into being. Nature has never been in balance, it is in fact careening through time colliding with the landscape.

Is there really a crisis? Would it really be a bad thing if the Earth were getting warmer? Warmer temperatures mean longer growing seasons. Longer growing seasons mean more food. And at a time when much of the world's population are going hungry, more food is a good thing.

Is carbon dioxide really such a bad thing? [18] Carbon dioxide occurs naturally. The major sources are volcanoes and respiration from animal life on Earth. As carbon dioxide increases, plant life, which uses carbon dioxide for photosynthesis, will grow more abundantly. Again, producing more food. There are even companies, which will install carbon dioxide in enhancement systems for commercial greenhouses, because it has been proven that increased carbon dioxide stimulates plant growth and larger crops.

Is carbon dioxide a greenhouse gas? Yes, it is. But it is not the only one. Water vapor is by far the most abundant greenhouse gas in the atmosphere. Methane is also a greenhouse gas, more potent than carbon dioxide. But you cannot tax water vapor, and methane is produced by termites and deep-sea microbes, which are far too intelligent life forms to submit to carbon taxes, so the global warming cultists have settled on carbon dioxide as the villain because a portion of carbon dioxide in the atmosphere can be traced to human activity.

How much atmospheric carbon dioxide comes from human activity? Not including respiration, human contribution to atmospheric carbon dioxide is 0.28% of the total atmospheric carbon dioxide.

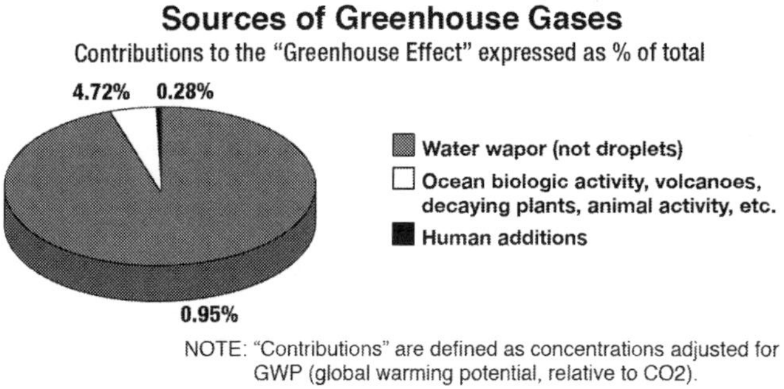

Source: www.geocraft.com/WVFossils/greenhouse_data.html

Now this may not seem like very much, and indeed it isn't. With volcanoes producing far more carbon dioxide than humans, one wonders what all the fuss is about regarding our cars and industry.

But the global warming cult has a handy explanation. The global warming cult likes to claim that natural sources of carbon dioxide are already balanced out by natural sinks for carbon dioxide. Volcanoes are offset by trees. The carbon dioxide emitted by sea life is absorbed by seaweed. By claiming that there is no natural counterpart to human-caused carbon dioxide the global warming cult tries to claim that 0.28% of atmospheric carbon dioxide contributed by human activity is upsetting the balance of nature. But as we pointed out before, there is no balance of nature. It is a romantic notion, but simply not reality.

Experiments with enhanced CO_2 in greenhouses confirm that as CO_2 levels rise, plants will grow larger, absorb more CO_2, driving levels back down again.

The Global Warming Fraud

So how do we know we are dealing with a fraud? As noted above, climate change is something that is supposed to happen. The world is always getting warmer or colder. The promotion of a change in the climate as a threat to humankind requiring the paying of taxes and submission to authority is a manufactured construct.

How do we know an agenda is involved? Simple. If the global warming alarmists were really only interested in the welfare of the Earth, one would expect them to be delirious with joy that the threat of anthropogenic global warming doesn't really exist after all. But quite to the contrary, those whose paychecks are dependent on the global warming industry are in a total panic to reassure us that, yes, there is a real danger, and it is all our fault!

Another reason we know anthropocentric global warming is a hoax is that scientific method is supposed to allow for others to double-check the work leading to the theory. In other words, starting with the same data and applying the same methods, I should get the same results. But in the case of anthropogenic global warming, this is impossible. The CRU (Climate Research Unit), in response to Freedom of Information requests for the raw data on which they based their dire predictions of doom, first stalled, then admitted they had destroyed the raw data! [19] We mere mortals are expected to simply take their word their conclusions are accurate. I have to wonder, with all the tens of millions of dollars in funding CRU enjoyed, why they could not purchase an extra hard drive to save that raw data!

In ancient times rulers ruled by whatever lie would convince the people that they needed to be ruled. One very common dodge was rule by divine right. "*I am your ruler, because God said so.*" But as mankind has evolved and become more sophisticated and understands that the idea of God is more a metaphor than reality, rulers intent on using deception to rule their people have had to come up with more convincing myths. "*Obey me, and I will save you from the Communists. Obey me, and I'll save you from the terrorists. Obey me, and I will save you from global warming.*" And so forth... So the push to sell global government on the basis of human-caused global warming is just another variation on the theme of "*I am the ruler, because the gods hath decreed it so.*" Maybe it's time for humans to evolve past this latest deception.

As for the actual evidence calling into question the claims of human-caused global warming, we can start with the very small percentage of atmospheric carbon dioxide actually created by human industry. The attempt by the Global Warming Cult to claim that natural carbon dioxide is not a problem because nature balances it out, but human-caused carbon dioxide is a threat, betrays the agenda of taking something that occurs naturally and focusing the blame for it onto humans in order to guilt them out of money and obedience.

We have previously documented [20] that temperature sensors used to generate the data that supports the claim of human-caused global warming have been cited in the outflow of building air conditioners and, in one notable instance, right next to a trash incinerator.[21] Clearly given that these are all sources of heat, the readings from these temperature sensors cannot be used to assume that we are measuring the temperature of anything other than air-conditioning outflow and the incineration of trash.

It has been documented and ruled in a British court of law [22] that Al Gore's film, *An Inconvenient Truth*, contained numerous factual errors. In one notable case, a film sequence showing the destruction of the polar caps turned out to be a fake – a computer-generated sequence from the science-fiction movie *The Day After Tomorrow*.

Much of the sensationalist media coverage of the issue of human-caused global warming has been exposed as a fraud. A story, which claimed polar bears were drowning because of global warming was exposed as a fraud, in which pictures of summer melt were presented as mid-winter scenes, along with the ludicrous claim that polar bears could not swim to shore to save their own lives.[23]

Then there was the recent video-taped admission by the head of Greenpeace [24] that the claim that Greenland would lose its ice in 20 years was merely a propaganda hoax!

The list of problems supposedly caused by human-caused global warming, from acne to prostitution, is endless, with more nonsense being added every day! [25]

The major problem that the global warming cultists have faced is that the Earth has actually been cooling for almost 12 years now. The global warming cultists attempted to re-brand by avoiding the term "global warming" and saying their agenda was to deal with "climate change." Not just any climate change of course, but sudden climate change, again the fault of humans, again requiring taxes and obedience to a global authority to solve. But re-branding as the Climate Change Cult did not secure the fact that the predictions for a warming globe were simply not panning out.

It was at this point that institutions dependent on funding to study human-caused global warming began to adjust their data in order to, as CRU put it, "conceal the decline." Otherwise, trust in the climate scientists was going to be undermined by the fact that they had obviously totally blown which way the temperatures of Earth were going, predicting that they were going up, when in fact they were demonstrably in decline.[26]

In one of the CRU emails [27] leaked by a whistleblower, Dr. Phil Jones, head of the CRU (until forced to step down) openly admits the Earth is getting cooler!

"This is from an Australian at BMRC (not Neville Nicholls). It began from the attached article. What an idiot. The scientific community would come down on me in no uncertain terms if I said the world had cooled from 1998. OK, it has, but it is only 7 years of data..."

Clearly from the above, Dr. Phil Jones is well aware that the Earth has been cooling for 7 (now 11) years and is clearly biased against allowing that information to be made public.

In the end, the most obvious evidence that the global warming cultists got it wrong is to look out your doors and windows this winter. Snow has come early to much of the Northern Hemisphere this [2009-2010] winter.[28] Ski resorts have opened early, and it looks to be a very hard winter. As of December 11th, 2009, 50% of the United States was under snow. On the same date last year [2008], only 29% of the United States was under snow.[29] The same global warming cultists who would point to temperature extremes 10 years ago as proof of their claims, now insist that early snows and frosts and ice should not be construed as evidence of global cooling. Clearly there is a bias at work here.

What is Really at Stake Here?

As I mentioned in the previous section, politicians seek to gain wealth and power and authority by taking something that occurs naturally, transforming it and promoting it as a crisis, and then selling the population a solution in exchange for higher taxes and increased authority over their lives.

Al Gore and his investors have created a crisis called human-caused global warming. They have created a product, literally out of thin air, called the carbon credit. This is essentially a license to pollute. And as experience in Europe has already shown, polluters will simply buy the license, and pass the cost on to consumers. The pollution will continue, has continued. The only real change is that goods and services cost more than they did before.

These so-called carbon credits will be bought from those who have too many, and resold to those who need more. This will require a brokerage, of which the only one currently in existence is owned by Al Gore and his investors, who stand to make billions of dollars from the trading of carbon credits. This is not unlike the manner in which Enron made billions of dollars off of the people of California by trading imbalances and electricity. It is not a coincidence that Enron's Ken Lay assisted Al Gore in setting up the structure for the trading of carbon credits. Al Gore is doing with carbon dioxide to the world what Ken lay did to California with electricity.

There is a huge amount of money at stake on convincing the people of the world that the Earth is getting warmer, that it is all their fault, and atonement lies with submitting to new taxation.

Those people still supporting anthropogenic global warming are dependent on funding to support their current positions. That funding is in turn dependent on the continuation of faith that AGW (anthropogenic global warming) is correct. After all, when Galileo proved that the Earth orbited the Sun, funding for continued research into epicycles vanished abruptly, along with tenures and the value of every degree issued in the field of epicycles.

The same applies here. With precious rare exception, every academic whose degree and funding is based on AGW is looking at a stark unemployment picture. In their minds, they are not fighting for scientific truth, they are fighting for their livelihood, and the proof is very simple. If their primary concern was really the long-term welfare of planet Earth, one would think the Global Warming Cult would be delighted to find out there really is no danger after all. But, as is clearly evident, the goal is to support the orthodoxy even against the revelation that their core scientific foundation is based on a fraud.

Quite a few people, including President Obama, are financially invested in the Global Carbon Credit scheme, in which licenses are issued to pollute, with the surplus units bought and sold through brokerages. Al Gore and his fellow investors have already spent $150 million to "sell" AGW. They will not walk away from that investment easily.

Beyond the researchers whose degrees and funding are dependent on the continuation of a perceived public threat, the media outlets and government officials who signed onto this campaign are now realizing that they have wagered their entire credibility on anthropogenic global warming at a time when their credibility was already strained from Saddam's "nookular" bombs, the economy, 9-11, etc., etc., etc. Climategate could well be the final nail in the coffin of the public's trust of media and government.

Just one example. Paul Hudson, BBC weatherman, who in October was sent Climategate emails, has been gagged by the BBC.[30]

Over and above the financial incentive, there is another agenda at work. There has been a push forward for the emergence of a global government for many years now. The plan to sell this new global oligarchy to the people of the world rests on three pillars. The first pillar is human-caused global warming, requiring submission to a global environmental authority. The second pillar is the global Swine Flu pandemic, requiring submission to a global health authority. The third pillar is the global financial crisis, requiring submission to a global banking authority. All three pillars are in serious trouble. If the pillar of human-caused global warming collapses, no doubt it will pull the other two down with it.

Clearly, there's a tremendous amount of political and financial power behind the selling of anthropogenic global warming to the people of the world. It is this political power which was able to provide Al Gore with an Academy Award for his documentary film, *An Inconvenient Truth*, even though that film has already been exposed as containing multiple factual errors. It was this same political power which obtained for Al Gore a Nobel Peace Prize, again for his documentary film, even though the deceptions had been exposed in a British court of law.[31]

So much money and political power has been invested in the myth of human-caused global warming that if human-caused global warming becomes exposed to the general population as a lie and a hoax, many well-known institutions of government and media will likely collapse from the scandal. The establishment is literally fighting for its life. And we should expect them to take any and all desperation measures to prolong and preserve their power and prestige and privilege.

This is a Street Brawl for Truth and Freedom

It is clear that government, the media, corporatized science, have quite literally bet the farm on selling the illusion of human-caused global warming as justification for global taxes and global government.

In order to bring about global government, simultaneously with creating the illusion of a need, they have to destroy the credibility of the regional governments, and we have seen a great deal of this lately. Now the oligarchs face an awkward choice. They have set the stage for a collapse of the national governments, and the global government they wish to install in its place may be collapsing right along with the myth of global warming.

Various governments and the media are so heavily invested in selling the illusion of human-caused global warming that, if that hoax is exposed, if the public becomes aware of the monstrous fraud involved, those institutions of government and media could very well be destroyed, and by their own hands.

Already we are seeing the organizers and perpetrators of this fraud trying to limit the damage from this exposure in several ways. The media is already hard at work attempting to dump the blame and scandal solely on the climate scientists, who after all were only doing what they were paid to do. This is not to say the scientists are not guilty. Quite the contrary, they deserve to be pilloried publicly and humiliated for their betrayal of the public trust. To say that their careers should be ended is an understatement. But in our haste to punish the scientists who assisted in the lies to the world, we must not forget that the scientists were working for somebody – for politicians such as Al Gore, for an agenda called global government, and for those who wanted to get rich by selling a fictitious product called carbon credit.

Yet another tactic being employed to limit the damage from Climategate is to insist that, even though the scientists responsible for the climate warming data have been exposed as holsters, the validity of the data itself must remain above question, above reproach. This of course is nonsense. If you hire a contractor to build a home, and discover afterwards that the contractor has a history of using substandard materials and sloppy workmanship, do you continue to believe the home he has built you is solid and durable and safe? Of course not. And yet the global warming cultists are demanding exactly this kind of naïveté from the public at large.

The latest spin is that if one questions the dogma of anthropocentric global warming, then one must be in favor of destroying the Earth. There is no middle ground. Another common propaganda tactic is to accuse those who question the veracity of the global warming cultists is to accuse them of receiving paychecks from oil companies. When one points out that the proponents of anthropogenic global warming are being paid for their work, one gets a "Hurrumph" of indignation. It's apparently acceptable for their side of the argument to be well-funded, because in their eyes they are the "good guys." Finally, there is the much-ballyhooed "precautionary principle," which states that one should never take any action that might cause harm even if that potential harm cannot be demonstrated or proven. In theory, such a prohibition should extend to any actions undertaken in support of the precautionary principle itself, but such suggestions get the usual "Hurrumph" of indignation. The cultists are really good at that.

So, is Climategate a fraud? Is Climategate a scientific scandal? No. Climategate is first and foremost a *political* scandal. More than that, it is a global political scandal that involves governments, media, institutionalized science, the banks, universities – indeed a vast cross-section of our ruling classes. It is more than a scandal – ***Climategate is a crime against humanity.*** And this is not an exaggeration. The goal of Climategate was to extract money from every human being on planet Earth in exchange for a nonexistent salvation from a nonexistent threat. The goal of Climategate was to trick every human being on planet Earth into accepting the yoke of a global oligarchy with no more legitimate claim to power than those who ruled by "divine right."

We are at a watershed moment. We may well see a transition to a new and better political structure for the entire world. But it will not be the one that has been designed for us. If nothing else, the ability for government and media to lie to the population of the world on such a vast scale is forever destroyed. Climategate will relegate all of the official stories of the governments of the United States and Great Britain, and indeed every government that took part in the human-caused global warming hoax, to the same level of credibility as Ramses carvings showing his victory over the Hittites. It will be seen as an historic joke by future generations.

But we are not there yet. The forces that have enslaved us with deception and fraud and hoax are desperate to hang onto their power and authority. They are busy coming up with new hoaxes and frauds to scare us back into obedience. And the media, well aware that they cannot report on the lies of Climategate without reporting their own complicity, are working hand in glove with government to reassert their ability to control what you think and when you think it.

So, what we, the free people of planet Earth, need to do is become the new mainstream media. The TV networks and other corporate media have been handed their marching orders to resell the illusion of human-caused climate change in any way, shape or form that will convince you to accept new taxes and the loss of your freedoms.

The only way the rest of the world is going to find out about Climategate is if you tell them. Because the TV and news magazines won't. If it's mentioned at all, it will be to trivialize and dismiss it and assure the world it really doesn't matter. BBC is still reporting Climategate as just another computer crime. This is like reporting Watergate as just another burglary!

We have collected together a vast body of evidence calling into question the legitimacy of the claims of human-caused global warming. We have collected together a vast body of evidence proving fraud and deception on the part of the global warming cult. Please forward this information to everybody you know. Time is of the essence.

Remember, global government is what Hitler wanted. Global government is what Napoleon wanted. Global government is what Alexander the Great wanted. Global government is what the Roman Caesars wanted.

Climategate may well prove to be the final fight in the war between those who would rule us with lies and those who wish to live with truth. Climategate makes it clear that, yes, there really are massive conspiracies between government and the media to mislead the general public. You cannot pretend they don't exist: one is right there before you, staked out naked on the ground, exposed for all to marvel at! I leave it as an exercise for the reader to decide how many other such deceptions form what we think we know of the world and of history.

There are two paths into the future. Along one lies freedom and truth and prosperity for the people. Along the other lies a socialist dictatorship, born in deception, unable and unwilling to tolerate dissent, and dedicated to robbing the poor to give to the rich.

You need to decide which future you wish to live in. And you need to decide what you will do about it.

Published in issue 8 of The Dot Connector magazine (March-April 2010).

The Marijuana Conspiracy

The reason hemp is illegal

Doug Yurchey

They say marijuana is dangerous. Pot is *not* harmful to the human body or mind. Marijuana does *not* pose a threat to the general public. Marijuana is very much a danger to the oil companies, alcohol, tobacco industries and a large number of chemical corporations. Big businesses, with plenty of dollars and influence, have suppressed the truth from the people. The truth is, if marijuana was utilized for its vast array of commercial products, it would create an industrial atomic bomb! The super rich have conspired to spread misinformation about the plant that, if used properly, would ruin their companies.

Where did the word 'marijuana' come from? In the mid 1930s, the M-word was created to tarnish the good image and phenomenal history of the hemp plant – as you will read. The facts cited here, with references, are generally verifiable in the *Encyclopaedia Britannica* which was printed on hemp paper for 150 years:

• All schoolbooks were made from hemp or flax paper until the 1880s. (Jack Frazier. *Hemp Paper Reconsidered*. 1974.)

• It was legal to pay taxes with hemp in America from 1631 until the early 1800s. (*LA Times*. Aug. 12, 1981.)

• *Refusing to grow hemp* in America during the 17th and 18th centuries *was against the law*! You could be jailed in Virginia for refusing to grow hemp from 1763 to 1769 (G. M. Herdon. *Hemp in Colonial Virginia*).

• George Washington, Thomas Jefferson and other founding fathers *grew hemp*. (Washington and Jefferson Diaries. Jefferson smuggled hemp seeds from China to France then to America.)

• Benjamin Franklin owned one of the first paper mills in America, and it processed hemp. Also, the War of 1812 was fought over hemp. Napoleon wanted to cut off Moscow's export to England. (Jack Herer. *Emperor Wears No Clothes.*)

• For thousands of years, 90% of all ships' sails and rope were made from hemp. The word *"canvas"* is Dutch for *cannabis.* (*Webster's New World Dictionary.*)

• 80% of all textiles, fabrics, clothes, linen, bed sheets, etc., were made from hemp until the 1820s, with the introduction of the cotton gin.

• The first Bibles, maps, charts, Betsy Ross's flag, the first drafts of the Declaration of Independence and the Constitution were made from hemp. (*U.S. Government Archives.*)

• The first crop grown in many states was hemp. 1850 was a peak year for Kentucky producing 40,000 tons. Hemp was the largest cash crop until the 20th century. (*State Archives.*)

• Oldest known records of hemp farming go back 5000 years in China, although hemp industrialization probably goes back to ancient Egypt.

• Rembrandt's, Van Gogh's, Gainsborough's, as well as most early canvas paintings, were principally painted on hemp linen.

• In 1916, the U.S. Government predicted that by the 1940s all paper would come from hemp and that no more trees need to be cut down. Government studies report that 1 acre of hemp equals 4.1 acres of trees. Plans were in the works to implement such programs. (*U.S. Department of Agriculture Archives.*)

• Quality paints and varnishes were made from hemp seed oil until 1937. 58,000 tons of hemp seeds were used in America for paint products in 1935. (*Sherman Williams Paint Co. testimony before the U.S. Congress against the 1937 Marijuana Tax Act.*)

• Henry Ford's first *Model-T* was built to run on *hemp gasoline,* and the car itself was *constructed from hemp*! On his large estate, Ford was photographed among his hemp fields. The car, "grown from the soil," had hemp plastic panels whose impact strength was 10 times stronger than steel. (*Popular Mechanics,* 1941.)

• In 1938, hemp was called *"Billion Dollar Crop."* It was the first time a cash crop had a business potential to exceed a billion dollars. (*Popular Mechanics,* Feb. 1938.)

• *Mechanical Engineering Magazine* (Feb. 1938) published an article entitled "The Most Profitable and Desirable Crop that Can be Grown." It stated that if hemp was cultivated using 20th century technology, it would be the single largest agricultural crop in the U.S. and the rest of the world.

The following information comes directly from the United States Department of Agriculture's 1942 14-minute film encouraging and instructing "patriotic American farmers" to grow 350,000 acres of hemp each year for the war effort:

"... *[When] Grecian temples were new, hemp was already old in the service of mankind. For thousands of years, even then, this plant had been grown for cordage and cloth in China and elsewhere in the East. For centuries prior to about 1850, all the ships that sailed the western seas were rigged with hempen rope and sails. For the sailor, no less than the hangman, hemp was indispensable...*

Now with Philippine and East Indian sources of hemp in the hands of the Japanese ... American hemp must meet the needs of our Army and Navy as well as of our industries...

The Navy's rapidly dwindling reserves. When that is gone, American hemp will go on duty again; hemp for mooring ships; hemp for tow lines; hemp for tackle and gear; hemp for countless naval uses both on ship and shore. Just as in the days when Old Ironsides sailed the seas victorious with her hempen shrouds and hempen sails. Hemp for victory!"

Certified proof from the Library of Congress, found by the research of Jack Herer, refutes claims of other government agencies that the 1942 USDA film *Hemp for Victory* did not exist.

Hemp cultivation and production do not harm the environment. The USDA Bulletin #404 concluded that hemp produces four times as much pulp with at least four to seven times less pollution.

From *Popular Mechanics*, February 1938:

"*It has a short growing season... It can be grown in any state... The long roots penetrate and break the soil to leave it in perfect condition for the next year's crop. The dense shock of leaves, 8 to 12 feet above the ground, chokes out weeds... Hemp, this new crop can add immeasurably to American agriculture and industry.*"

In the 1930s, innovations in farm machinery would have caused an industrial revolution when applied to hemp. This single resource could have created millions of new jobs generating thousands of quality products.

Hemp, if not made illegal, would have brought America out of the Great Depression!

The Conspiracy

William Randolph Hearst (Citizen Kane) and the Hearst Paper Manufacturing Division of Kimberly Clark owned vast acreage of timberlands. The Hearst Company supplied most paper products. Patty Hearst's grandfather, a destroyer of nature for his own personal profit, stood to lose billions because of hemp.

In 1937, *DuPont* patented the processes to make plastics from oil and coal. *DuPont*'s Annual Report urged stockholders to invest in its new petrochemical division. Synthetics such as plastics, cellophane, celluloid, methanol, nylon, rayon, Dacron, etc., could now be made from oil. Natural hemp industrialization would have ruined over 80% of *DuPont*'s business.

Andrew Mellon became Hoover's Secretary of the Treasury and *DuPont*'s primary investor. He appointed his future nephew-in-law, Harry J. Anslinger, to head the Federal Bureau of Narcotics and Dangerous Drugs.

Secret meetings were held by these financial tycoons. Hemp was declared dangerous and a threat to their billion dollar enterprises. For their dynasties to remain intact, hemp had to go. These men took an obscure Mexican slang word: "*marijuana*" and pushed it into the consciousness of America.

Media Manipulation

A media blitz of 'yellow journalism' raged in the late 1920s and 1930s. Hearst's newspapers ran stories emphasizing the horrors of marijuana. The menace of marijuana made headlines. Readers learned that it was responsible for everything from car accidents to loose morality.

Films like *Reefer Madness* (1936), *Marijuana: Assassin of Youth* (1935) and *Marijuana: The Devil's Weed* (1936) were propaganda designed by these industrialists to create an enemy. Their purpose was to gain public support so that anti-marijuana laws could be passed.

Examine the following quotes from *The Burning Question*, aka *Reefer Madness*:

- a violent narcotic;
- acts of shocking violence;
- incurable insanity;
- soul-destroying effects;
- under the influence of the drug he killed his entire family with an ax;

- more vicious, more deadly even than these soul-destroying drugs (heroin, cocaine) is the menace of marijuana!

Reefer Madness did not end with the usual "The End." The film concluded with these words plastered on the screen: *"Tell your children."*

In the 1930s, people were very naive, even to the point of ignorance. The masses were like sheep waiting to be led by the few in power. They did not challenge authority. If the news was in print or on the radio, they believed it had to be true. They told their children, and their children grew up to be the parents of the baby-boomers.

On April 14, 1937, the prohibitive Marijuana Tax Law, or the bill that outlawed hemp, was directly brought to the House Ways and Means Committee. This committee is the only one that can introduce a bill to the House floor without it being debated by other committees. The Chairman of the U.S. Senate, Ways and Means Committee, at the time, Robert Doughton, was a *DuPont* supporter. He insured that the bill would pass Congress.

Dr. James Woodward, a physician and attorney, testified too late on behalf of the American Medical Association. He told the committee that the reason the AMA had not denounced the Marijuana Tax Law sooner was that the Association had just discovered that marijuana was hemp.

Few people, at the time, realized that the deadly menace they had been reading about on Hearst's front pages was in fact passive hemp. The AMA understood cannabis to be a *medicine* found in numerous healing products sold over the last hundred years.

In September of 1937, hemp became illegal. The most useful crop known became a drug, and our planet has been suffering ever since.

Congress banned hemp because it was said to be the most violence-causing drug known. Harry Anslinger, head of the Drug Commission for 31 years, promoted the idea that marijuana made users act extremely violent. In the 1950s, under the Communist threat of McCarthyism, Anslinger then said the exact opposite: marijuana will pacify you so much that soldiers would not want to fight.

Today, our planet is in desperate trouble. Earth is suffocating as large tracts of rain forests disappear. Pollution, poisons and chemicals are killing people. These great problems could be reversed if we industrialized hemp. Natural biomass could provide all of the planet's energy needs that are currently supplied by fossil fuels. We have consumed 80% of our oil and gas reserves. We need a renewable resource. Hemp could be the solution.

The Wonder Plant

Hemp has a higher quality fiber than wood fiber. Far fewer caustic chemicals are required to make paper from hemp than from trees. Hemp paper does not turn yellow and is very durable. The plant grows quickly to maturity in a season, where trees take a lifetime.

All plastic products should be made from hemp seed oil. Hempen plastics are biodegradable! Over time, they would break down and not harm the environment. Oil-based plastics, the ones we are very familiar with, help ruin nature. They do not break down and will do great harm in the future. The process to produce the vast array of natural (hempen) plastics will not ruin the rivers as *DuPont* and other petrochemical companies have done. Ecology does not fit in with the plans of the oil industry and the political machine. Hemp products are safe and natural.

Medicines should be made from hemp. We should go back to the days when the AMA supported cannabis cures. "Medical Marijuana" is given out legally to only a handful of people while the rest of us are forced into a system that relies on chemicals. Pot is only healthy for the human body.

World hunger could end. A large variety of food products can be generated from hemp. The seeds contain one of the highest sources of protein in nature. *Also:* They have two essential fatty acids that clean your body of cholesterol. These essential fatty acids are not found anywhere else in nature! Consuming pot seeds is the best thing you could do for your body. Eat uncooked hemp seeds.

Clothes should be made from hemp. Hemp clothing is extremely strong and durable over time. You could hand clothing, made from pot, down to your grandchildren. Today, there are American companies that make hemp clothing, usually 50% hemp. Hemp fabrics should be everywhere. Instead, they are almost underground. Superior hemp products are not allowed to advertise on fascist television. Kentucky, once the top hemp producing state, made it *illegal to wear* hemp clothing! Can you imagine being thrown into jail for wearing quality jeans?

The world is crazy. But that does not mean you have to join the insanity. Get together. Spread the news. Tell people, and that includes your children, the truth. Use hemp products. Eliminate the word 'marijuana.' Realize the history that created it. Make it politically incorrect to say or print the M-word. Fight against the propaganda (designed to favor the agenda of the super rich) and the bullshit. Hemp must be utilized in the future. We need a clean energy source to save our planet. *Industrialize hemp!*

The liquor, tobacco and oil companies fund more than a million dollars a day to Partnership for a Drug-Free America and other similar agencies. We have all seen their commercials. Now, their motto is: "*It's more dangerous than we thought.*" Lies from the powerful corporations, that began with Hearst, are still alive and well today.

The brainwashing continues. Now, the commercials say: If you buy a joint, you contribute to murders and gang wars. The latest anti-pot commercials say: If you buy a joint, you are promoting *terrorism*! The new enemy has paved the road to brainwash you any way they see fit.

There is only one enemy: the friendly people you pay your taxes to, the war-makers and nature destroyers. With your funding, they are killing the world right in front of your eyes.

Half a million deaths each year are caused by tobacco. Half a million deaths each year are caused by alcohol. No one has ever died from smoking pot!!

In the entire history of the human race, not one death can be attributed to cannabis. Our society has outlawed grass but condones the use of the *killers*: tobacco and alcohol. Hemp should be declassified and placed in *drug* stores to relieve stress. Hardening and constriction of the arteries are bad, but hemp usage actually enlarges the arteries, which is a healthy condition. We have been so conditioned to think that smoking is harmful. That is *not* the case for passive pot.

Ingesting THC, hemp's active agent, has a positive effect: relieving asthma and glaucoma. A joint tends to alleviate the nausea caused by chemotherapy. You are able to eat on hemp. This is a healthy state of being.

[ONE PERSONAL NOTE. *During the pregnancy of my wife, she was having some difficulty gaining weight. We were in the hospital. A nurse called us to one side and said:* "Off the record, if you smoke pot ... you'd get something called the munchies and you'll gain weight." *I swear that is a true story.*]

The stereotype for a pothead is similar to a drunk, bubble-brain. Yet, the truth is one's creative abilities can be enhanced under its influence. The perception of time slightly slows and one can become more sensitive. You can more appreciate all arts, be closer to nature and generally *feel* more under the influence of cannabis. It is, in fact, the exact opposite state of mind and body as the drunken state. You can be more aware with pot.

The pot plant is an *alien* plant. There is physical evidence that cannabis is not like the most of other plants on this planet. One could conclude that it was brought here for the benefit of humanity. Hemp is one of a *very few* plants where the males appear one way and the females appear very different, physically!

No one ever speaks of males and females in regard to the plant kingdom because plants do not show their sexes. Except for cannabis. To determine what sex a certain, normal, earthly plant is, you have to look internally, at its DNA. A male blade of grass (physically) looks exactly like a female blade of grass. The hemp plant has an intense sexuality. Growers know to kill the males before they fertilize the females. Yes, folks, the most potent pot comes from "horny females."

The reason this amazing, very sophisticated, ET plant from the future is illegal has nothing to do with how it physically affects us.

Pot is illegal because billionaires want to remain billionaires!

"And I will raise up for them a plant of renown, and they shall be no more consumed with hunger in the land." – Ezekiel 34:29.

P.S. I think the word *"drugs"* should not be used as an umbrella-word that covers all chemical agents. Drugs have come to be known as something *bad.* Are you aware there are *legal* drugstores?! Yep, in every city. Unbelievable. Each so-called drug should be considered individually. Cannabis is a medicine and not a drug. We should *dare* to speak the *truth* no matter what the law is.

Published in issue 2 of The Dot Connector magazine (March-April 2009).

Sinister Forces in American Political Witchcraft

Interview with Peter Levenda

Kerry Cassidy and Bill Ryan

Peter Levenda came to our notice as the author of the powerful, compelling, and well-researched *Sinister Forces* – the trilogy which explores the links between the Nazis, the occult, mind control and modern American politics and asks uncomfortable questions about what forces underlie and control global events. Peter Levenda was researching the Nazi connection to American politics and secret societies as early as the Nixon administration. He summarized his findings in a highly regarded book called *Unholy Alliance*. These same dark forces surfaced during the administration of George W. Bush and remain as an important question for the direction of America with Barack Obama.

We feel fortunate to have stumbled upon Peter Levenda's impeccable research, which connects the dots between the agenda of the Illuminati, the Nazi influence within black projects and the US government, and the role of the occult and mind control in what is becoming the new world we are living in where the very foundation of freedom is being attacked and curtailed, threatening our humanity at every juncture.

KERRY CASSIDY: Peter, could you start by giving the reader, basically, a background on where you come from, how you came at this material?

PETER LEVENDA: Well, I tried, back in the 1970s, during the Watergate era, to write a book that was going to explore the relationship between religion and politics, which is a nexus that's always fascinated me. We tend in the United States to think of them as two separate entities. But during Watergate I began to see a lot of the same personalities crop up that we had run across during, oh, the Kennedy assassinations and all of that, and I started to see deeper and deeper parallels.

So there was a book that came out in 1960, long before Watergate, called *The Morning of the Magicians*. It was written by two Frenchmen, Pauwels and Bergier, and it talked a great deal in there about a Nazi/occult connection, but it was not documented at all. And I thought: "*That would make a great chapter* [Kerry laughs] *in the book that I was planning. Let me write something about the Nazis and religion, or Nazis and occultism or mysticism.*"

And I went down to the National Archives in Washington, D.C. This was right at the height of Watergate. Nixon was still in power. He was about to leave. It was a month or two before he left, so the whole thing was at fever pitch in Washington.

But, oblivious to that in a sense, I was at the National Archives looking at captured German documents. As I was in the National Archives, the archivist there, a very famous archivist – anyone who studied the Nazis back in the '70s and '80s would have known about Dr. Wolfe – when he found out what I was trying to do, he suggested that I look at the records of an organization called the SS Ahnenerbe, which was actually a division of the SS that was specifically concerned with occult and mystical research. I was stunned.

He led me to the microfilm rolls. I started going through the machines. And here I realized – my jaw dropped – I was looking at the actual documentation of a full-fledged Nazi program to investigate occultism.

Other authors had talked about a Nazi/occult connection. The book, *The Morning of the Magicians*, talked about it at length, but there was no documentation at all. And some of the other books that had come out at that time, for instance, *The Spear of Destiny*, and some of the others, talked extensively about this but there was no documentation.

So it seemed like speculation until suddenly I'm staring at all the documents – page after page after page of research in Tibet, Tibet expeditions. There was research to find the Holy Grail. There was all sorts of bizarre SS programs that were being financed heavily by the Nazis during World War Two.

So it got me thinking that maybe there is a lot of documentation in the world. Maybe you *can* find evidence of all of this without having to speculate too much. So the Nazi documentation got me very excited.

I lived in New York City at the time. I'm from New York City. I was talking to a lot of friends of mine who had their roots in Latin America and South America. I read a book by Ladislas Farago, called *Aftermath*, which is about the survival of war criminals, Nazi war criminals, in South America.

And I came across the mentioning of a weird establishment in Chile, called "Colonia Dignidad," the Colony of Righteousness. This was supposed to be a kind of Nazi safe-house which was also a weird religious group, high up in the Andes Mountains. And I thought: *"This is just too good to pass up."* So here not only do I have the documentation from World War Two, but now I have a real live Nazi sanctuary in South America, which is also a religious operation, which is exactly what I was writing about.

So I decided to go to Chile – this was in 1979 – and see this place for myself. This was during the time of the Pinochet dictatorship. There was martial law in the country, but I managed to make my way down to a small town halfway down the coast of Chile, called Parral. And close to this small town is the colony, Colonia Dignidad.

I managed to go up there. The story is told at length in my book, *Unholy Alliance*. But I managed to go there on a Sunday morning in June of 1979, and I was briefly detained. I was kept there. I was forbidden to leave. My passport was taken. The film was taken out of my camera.

I was told by the Germans... These were Germans, these were not Chilenos, these were not Spanish people – I was told by the Germans that I was not welcome in the country, that I had to leave Chile immediately.

And as I was allowed to leave, which was touch-and-go for a while, all the way back to Santiago, to the capital where I had my hotel room, I was stopped along the way. I was in a bus and I was stopped along the way by troops who had set up roadblocks, who were making sure that I was on that bus. When I got back to my hotel room, there was a note waiting for me that said I was on the next plane, that a reservation had been made.

So the amount of influence that the Nazi network had in 1979... 1979 was so many years after the end of World War Two, you know. We're talking 25 years later. They still had such great influence in a country so far away as Chile that I began to see there was a lot more going on than I even suspected. And that eventually became *Unholy Alliance*.

I began to see the connections between governments in Bolivia, Chile, Argentina, Paraguay, an extensive Nazi network, a lot of money that had left the Third Reich when the Nazis had lost the war.

I began to realize that the Nazi Party was not a political party the way we understand political parties, but that the Nazi Party was a cult. If you look at it from that point of view, you can understand the true nature of this kind of evil, because the Nazi Party is … they're not going to go away simply because they lost the war.

The old war criminals who escaped – and some of them are still alive, a few of them have died recently in South America, in Chile and Argentina – they have their followers. They have their philosophy, their ideology.

BILL RYAN: Forgive me for interrupting you, Peter… but it sounds implicit in what you're saying that they have support from deep within the governments of those South American countries.

P.L.: Sure. I mean, it depends on which regime is in power at any given time. But let's take the example of Bolivia. Klaus Barbie, who was the "Butcher of Lyon" in France, who was a man responsible for all sorts of war crimes in France, at one point became the chief of the secret police of Bolivia. I mean, he had a federally appointed position in that government.

Walter Rauff lived for a very long time in Chile. Walter Rauff was the man who designed the mobile gas chambers, the vans that were used to re-channel the exhaust into the vans to kill prisoners. I mean, all of these people found safe haven, not only in South America, but in the Middle East and in Asia as well, and to a certain extent in Australia.

K.C.: And in the United States as well.

P.L.: Absolutely. Certainly. Of course we've had many cases here in the United States of war criminals that we've found, uncovered, and occasionally shipped back.

A famous one, which got me very involved in the story, was the man who for a long time was the head of the Romanian Orthodox Church in the United States. Here was an Archbishop who during World War Two had been a member of the… what was the name… the Iron Cross? The Iron Arrow, I think, a Romanian Nazi organization, who had tortured prisoners. Here was a man who was a devoted Nazi, who, after the war was over, fled to the United States, and although he had no seminarial training as far as I've been able to uncover, he managed to take over one branch of the Romanian Orthodox Church in our country, in the Midwest, and was not even discovered until maybe 20 years ago, when he was forced to leave the country.

So, yeah, we've helped a lot of people escape. The Catholic Church also, to a certain extent, was involved in that, in an operation called *Caritas*, during World War Two, which provided Vatican passports to help some of the more famous war criminals escape to South America. So there was a lot of collaboration.

And even in our own country, in the United States, we had *Operation Paperclip*, in which we brought Nazi scientists over to help with our space program, among other things.

So that got me working on what eventually became *Sinister Forces*. I began to wonder how was it that we in the United States could have sold our souls so easily to something as heinous as a criminal organization like the SS, and to the Nazis in general, to bring their scientists over here, to make them work for us, and really to give them great jobs, to give them positions in our industry.

Walter Dornberger is an example, who held a job on the board of directors of Bell Helicopter. All sorts of people. People who worked for the Space Medicine Program in Texas, at Randolph Air Force Base. There's a very big story there.

K.C.: Right. And that has tentacles that go to the whole mind control aspect. I think that you cover that really wonderfully in *Sinister Forces*. I mean, I can't imagine what you do in *Book Two* and *Book Three*, but I have to say that that's really a huge story.

P.L.: Well, I develop the same ideas. In *Book Two* I focus a lot on the Charles Manson family, as a kind of quintessential example of what sinister forces might be from the behavior modification/mind control aspect. And then in *Book Three* I sort of lay out what I think is the whole story and how this works. I connect serial killers to mind control operations and try to understand.

I mean, our country, the CIA in particular in the 1950s, 1960s, all the way up through until about Watergate, until the 1970s and the Rockefeller investigations, was involved in one of the most bizarre experiments of modern times. I mean, here we were, trying to figure out how the human consciousness worked, how to understand memory, volition. How do we erase a person's memory, implant new memories? How do we make a person do something they would not ordinarily do – for instance, commit an assassination? And then forget about it and not know why they did it? I mean, this was something like a medieval king, you might think, hiring alchemists and magicians, you know, to contact the other world. We were doing that in the 1950s and 1960s, and probably still are today.

We have operations in which we are trying to understand how the mind works and then to control it. Like a sorcerer's apprentice, our intelligence agencies stuck their fingers into human consciousness and started playing around with the contents.

B.R.: What's the answer to your own question, Peter, which you posed just a couple of minutes ago? About how... I think the words you used were: Were there evil forces at work in America during the Second World War? Or was this something that was opportunistic because they realized the magic that they certainly held in their hands and thought that they could use this to their own ends, and it was too great a temptation to resist?

P.L.: Well, I think, as usual, the causes take place on different levels simultaneously. I think to point in one direction only might be a mistake. I think sometimes it's desired that we do look in a certain direction and not look in another one – the idea of misdirection.

I talk about *Sinister Forces.* I mean, that's the title of my series, and I took that title from Watergate because that's how I started this research. And "sinister forces" were blamed for that famous 18.5 minute tape gap on the Oval Office tapes, on Nixon's office tapes, where there was suddenly a big gap and no one knew what he had said.

I think it was Alexander Haig or Buzhardt who had said the tape, the hissing sound on the tape, was the result of "sinister forces." And I liked that idea, that there was something darker at work.

I think that in many cases what we see around us is theater, a kind of theater, and that there are forces that are deeper, darker, less visible, manipulating events. Or I like to think that what we call coincidence and synchronicity is evidence of the action of a darker force, or a deeper force.

B.R.: And are these forces also much more ancient? Because of course there are many researchers, possibly yourself, who conclude that this whole thing, this whole dark agenda, had its roots 2,000 or even 3,000 years ago, and it's been growing steadily since then.

K.C.: Well, actually in your book you're talking about going back into the mounds in America, so you're going back thousands if not millions of years. Right?

P.L.: Certainly.

K.C.: And there's also the allusion to Egypt and the pyramids. And you're talking about, you actually have to get to possible off-world cultures, and how humanity began on this planet, when you go that deep, really.

P.L.: Well, when I started looking at the burial mounds... The idea of the Indian burial mounds came to me sheerly by accident, because I was researching Manson and I decided to go where Charles Manson had grown up, which was a town called Ashland, in Kentucky.

I was struck by the fact that there were Indian burial mounds right in the center of town. And I started to research that, wondering what did that mean? I had never really come across this before. This was brand new to me. I started to look at the fact that these mounds are all over the United States, especially east of the Mississippi, but also west of the Mississippi to a certain extent.

I was struck by the fact that there was actually an ancient civilization in America, in North America, that we have no clue about. It was just as ancient as anything that was taking place in the Middle East. The earthworks that they built were in some cases more grand and a lot larger than the pyramids, and we know so little about it.

I began to look at America as a kind of haunted house, and I began to ask myself: "*What forces are there really at work here?*" The coincidences that we come across, especially a conspiracy theorist... Anybody who begins to investigate – the Kennedy assassination is probably the most famous example – will come across dozens and then hundreds and then maybe thousands of "coincidental" connections, between people, places, and events, which drives them crazy.

A regular historian, a mainstream historian's going to say: "*Well, that was a coincidence; and that was a coincidence; and that was a coincidence,*" and dismiss them all because he cannot see a real cause-and-effect relationship. But to me, and it happens to all of us who investigate these things, we find ourselves bedeviled by these coincidences.

I was researching *Sinister Forces* for a while in Asia. I was in Southeast Asia, in remote areas, and I would walk into a second-hand bookstore and find books that I needed for my research. They were books on Charles Manson, or something that I had never heard of before. Scholarly texts would suddenly appear; or texts would appear that had been written and printed privately by someone involved with the group that I call "The Nine."

All of this stuff would fall into my hands even though I was in the middle of nowhere, nowhere near any sort of academic structure, nowhere near a Barnes and Noble bookstore or anything like that, [*laughs*] but just really in the middle of nowhere.

So, the multiplication of these events, to me, is an indication that something else is at work, that maybe we need a quantum consciousness approach to history itself, not just to our own minds in a kind of theoretical way or a spiritual…

K.C.: Absolutely. Absolutely.

P.L.: History… Yep.

K.C.: You're talking about [Andrija] Puharich… And that opens a can of worms around the mind control and how the mind control seems to stem from those early beginnings and the consciousness that supposedly Puharich actually got into contact – those "Nine" people – of which there are people that have written books since then and supposedly gotten involved in contact with, if not those intelligences, then others. Some call them the *Giza Intelligences*. So it's all going back omewhere there, as well.

P.L.: Well, yeah. I mean, if you begin with Puharich, you can see the contours of what I'm talking about quite clearly, because here was a man who was a researcher into the paranormal, but he was also a captain in the US Army and a medial doctor, all of these things all together. And this was all during the Korean War.

Here was a man who was giving lectures to the military on how to weaponize ESP [extrasensory perception], you know, how to use man's telekinetic and telepathic powers as a weapon in the fight in the Cold War.

At the same time, he's holding a séance, or a series of séances, at a farmhouse in Maine to which he's invited a handful of people. But the people he's invited are some of the wealthiest families in America, the most powerful families in America, "blue-bloods", I mean, who are descended from the signers of the Declaration of Independence.

The thing that fascinates me about this is that this is thoroughly documented stuff. There's no speculation about this at all. Anyone can go and look it up and find out for themselves that these people did meet, they conducted the séance, they were in contact with some extraterrestrial or supernatural group of beings which called themselves "The Nine."

And we're talking about people who were also tangentially involved in the Kennedy assassination, which would take place ten, fifteen years after these events. I mean, it's stunning. I mean, you ask yourself: "*What is the connection? How could this possibly be?*"

B.R.: Yes. What did you think of Picknett and Prince's book, *The Stargate Conspiracy*, that you must have read as part of your research?

P.L.: I did read *The Stargate Conspiracy* and I wanted to shout at Picknett and Prince: "*Just go a little bit further! Go just a little bit more and you will see the connections right back to the Kennedy assassination.*"

I was thrilled that they were writing about these events, about "The Nine" also. They were writing about Puharich. They had mentioned him. They had mentioned this group, but they had not drawn the connection. They had not connected the dots between, for instance, Arthur Young, who was a prominent member of "The Nine," a man who invented the Bell Helicopter, which I had mentioned just a little while ago as having been involved with Nazi scientists…

B.R.: When you talk about "The Nine," are you talking about a human group, or an off-world group? Or is this an allusion to two groups of nine?

P.L.: Well, when I talk about "The Nine," I'm focusing first on the human group because those are the names of the people that we know. But of course they were considered to be the Earthly representatives of this spiritual or extraterrestrial group that called themselves "The Nine."

B.R.: OK. What is that Earthly group of nine?

P.L.: Well, "The Nine" included families – for instance, Arthur Young and his wife, Ruth Forbes Paine Young, who is a relative of John Kerry's, as a matter of fact – John Forbes Kerry. So we have Arthur Young and his wife, Ruth Forbes Paine Young.

We have a DuPont, we have an Astor, all as part of this group, as well as Puharich. So the Astor family was there – a very wealthy American and British family, the Astors. Of course, everyone knows the Astors and the Waldorf Astoria, etcetera, etcetera. John Jacob Astor was on the *Titanic*. So we have the Astor family.

We have the DuPonts, of course – extremely powerful, wealthy, influential American family. And we have the Forbes – as in *Forbes Magazine* – Steve Forbes, and all of that. That family was represented.

Her [Arthur Young's wife's] name was Ruth Forbes Paine. Paine was one of the original signers of the Declaration of Independence. She is a direct descent along that line by marriage. And Arthur Young himself, the inventor of the Bell Helicopter.

So you have a family grouping here of some of the most aristocratic family names in America. If we had royalty, they would be DuPonts and Astors, Forbes and Paines.

B.R.: Did they call themselves "The Nine"? Or is this your term for them? I mean, did they have an agenda, or some kind of thesis, or reason for being together and recognized as a group of that size?

P.L.: Well, they called themselves "The Nine" in this fashion. They held a séance. Puharich was conducting a séance. He had a medium from India, a Dr. Vinod, and Vinod was in telepathic communication with a group of beings that was somehow in space, hovering over the Earth, and there were nine of them.

And they told the group of nine individuals: "*We are nine, and you are nine, therefore you are the Brahmins who are going to bring a new wave of enlightenment, or a new wave of evolution to the planet. We're going to use you as our vehicle for causing this kind of spiritual evolution, this jumpstarting of evolution, if you will.*"

K.C.: And this was also a take-off on basically what the Illuminati had been, their philosophy since the beginning of the group that we call the Illuminati, of which these families are all part?

P.L.: Well, that's the implication. I mean, otherwise... Why are these people, as I said before, some of the wealthiest individuals in the United States, in Maine, in a barn, in the woods, on New Year's Eve, when they could have been anywhere else in the world – they had the money, they had the wherewithal, they had the connections – instead, they're holding séances in the freezing cold, in the winter, in this barn? What is the motivation for this? What is the purpose? How did they know each other? We don't know so much about that. We know that Puharich was the guy bringing them all together for the séance and they willingly went and took part in this endeavor, not just once but several times.

So, their motivation, on their own? I don't know. I wouldn't want to speculate except to say we're talking about the most powerful people in our country at the time.

B.R.: And the analogy that you're drawing here is that there's good evidence that the Nazis were doing something similar, both before and during the war, and you're saying that powerful individuals from powerful families in a powerful nation-state are suddenly doing the same thing several decades later.

P.L.: Well, yes. I mean, less than ten years later. If we count the end of World War Two as 1945, these people were meeting in the early 1950s.

And what Himmler was doing, himself? I went and visited in Germany the castle that he had renovated, called Wewelsburg. It's near the town of

Paderborn. And this castle was developed by him to be a kind of Vatican for the SS. It was going to be their spiritual headquarters. He was conducting very similar rituals there. He had duplicated a kind of "Roundtable", a sort of Arthurian, Camelot kind of idea. There would be 12 knights around it, which were the highest ranking SS officers. They would gather in meditation at this table, in a room which was directly over a crypt, and in the crypt would be placed urns containing the ashes of SS officers as they died, the high ranking ones. There was special niche for each one. There were swastikas engraved in the floors, and the whole nine yards.

And so, the similar idea of meditation, of trying to contact supernatural beings to guide the SS, was now being duplicated by a group called "The Nine." And if we think in terms of race – you know the SS, like all the Nazis, were obsessed with racial purity – suddenly, with "The Nine" we have, as I said, the blue-blood of American families – DuPonts, Astors, Paines, Forbes. We have this gathering of the … for want of a better word, the most *racially acceptable*, to the Nazis, grouping in guided meditations in the woods, doing the same thing. Except they were not twelve in this case. They were nine, very specifically. So, I'm not trying to draw too close a connection between what the Nazis were doing and "The Nine." The practices were quite similar. It was a group séance. It was a meditation. It was something to do with evolution of the race. So you have a lot of the same themes.

K.C.: OK. But what you also, I think, continued to investigate was to find out where that information that they were receiving from "The Nine" went from there. Because I believe there is a trail that connects through SRI [Stanford Research Institute] and Hal Puthoff and Ingo Swann…

P.L.: Sure.

K.C.: … remote viewing, and actually circles back and also has to do with people that were involved in mind control, utilizing some of that information? And/or is it guiding, for example, the agenda of the Illuminati to this day?

P.L.: Well, it certainly did make that route that you just described, and the connective tissue in all of this, of course, is Andrija Puharich. He was the man largely credited with having discovered Uri Geller, for instance, the famous Israeli psychic. He brought Geller to SRI to be tested.

There was also a connection with SRI and that grouping, with the people at Jonestown. The connections are vast with all of this, and if you start pulling at the threads, you become extremely paranoid.

B.R.: What's the connection with Jonestown?

P.L.: Well, yes. In *Volume Two*, I have about 100 pages alone just on Jonestown, because the amount of work that has yet to be done just to decode that event is still leaning on us. We really know very little about what really happened at Jonestown.

Slowly but surely more and more information has been revealed over the last 20 years or so, some of it by a good friend of mine called Jim Hogan, an investigative journalist who spent a lot of time researching Jonestown and came up with some of the CIA documents to verify that Jim Jones himself was some kind of contract agent with the CIA. He had what's called a *201 File* at CIA. So we know there was a connection there.

But as far as the connection with SRI, I think it was Russell Targ – if I'm not mistaken, I believe it's Russell Targ who was the man who was involved with both Jonestown and SRI and Hal Puthoff.

K.C.: There's also the link back to Puharich as working for the CIA.

P.L.: Yes. As far as Uri Geller was concerned, Geller always said that Puharich was his handler for the CIA. He made that statement several times. But as far as SRI is concerned, Russell Targ, the physicist who was part of the SRI group, by his own admission, was involved with a group of Jonestown survivors. He was director of counseling at their Human Freedom Center in Berkeley and left them to join SRI to study psychic phenomena.

The group that he was working with, Elmer and Deanna Mertle, after he left them, a few weeks after Targ left them to join SRI, the Mertles were found dead, murdered execution-style in their home. So the connection between Targ, SRI, and Jonestown is definite. What it means, we don't know. But we do know that Targ worked with the Mertles, which was a group of survivors of the Jonestown massacre, people who had left the Jim Jones church, The People's Temple, and were trying to raise consciousness against it. They had written a book about The People's Temple, and Targ was working with them. He left to join SRI, and a couple of weeks later, the Mertles were dead, murdered execution-style.

K.C.: So you have to also say that with all of this what happens is some people will fall on working for the positive and some will be working actually for the negative agenda, within the fact that there are connections between these organizations. Because there is very definite connection between the CIA and SRI. And between Puharich and CIA. So you get all these connections with CIA. Gordon Novel, the Kennedy assassination.

All of these link back to the CIA. So it gets really convoluted. It's really fascinating... I know that you've studied the occult in great depth. Have you come to any conclusions? Are you going down some trails now that perhaps are not publicized?

P.L.: Well, not publicized to the point that I don't quite know how to explain all of this yet in any way that makes any kind of sense from an academic point of view, but it has occurred to me during this kind of research... As I mentioned before, I consider coincidence and synchronicity to be evidence of the operation of these forces.

I think that these forces are there, and I think that groups of human beings from time to time make a conscious effort to contact these forces, to manipulate them, to use them for their own advantages. I think that the CIA did that with *MKULTRA* and *Operation Bluebird* and all of the mind control experiments they did.

If you take a human being and try to manipulate their consciousness, you try to erase their memories, replace their memories, program them as assassins, as an example, then you're essentially initiating that human being. I mean, you're putting them through a kind of spiritual initiation, but with none of the safeguards, with none of the spiritual preparation that a person would normally go through to become protected against whatever demons are invoked in the process. So it was a very irresponsible, callous, cruel program that the CIA had undertaken at that time.

K.C.: Irresponsible or actually intentional? I mean, that's really the question, isn't it, of the heads of the CIA: if they knew what they were getting into? And they were invoking these negative forces, and bringing them into the bodies of programmed assassins, some of which are actually sleeper agents that may indeed be part of our society at the moment, sitting around waiting to be triggered. In essence, what you're looking at could be an intentional agenda. And that's where it gets very interesting when you're starting to look at the future and what we're actually faced with.

P.L.: Well, yeah. I mean, I think one of the good indications of just how bad it got was the man who was for a long time in charge of this program at the CIA, called Sydney Gottlieb, Dr. Sydney Gottlieb... When the *MKULTRA* project was "disbanded" by Richard Helms in the mid-1970s, Gottlieb went a little weird. He at one point became a Buddhist monk. He went to India. He tried to essentially pay for his sins. He wouldn't talk about this program anymore, but he became a kind of recluse and was obviously trying to live simply. He was living off the land. He was living in a farmhouse, I believe in Virginia, after he came back from India. He was a man who was shattered by the realizations of what he had done, by the sins that he had committed against other human beings.

So if the leader, if the creator, or the handmaiden of this operation felt that way, I wonder what the actual day-to-day perpetrators felt, the people who were actually involved in the day-to-day programming of these individuals.

I think there is a tremendous amount of evidence to suggest that Sirhan Sirhan was just exactly one of those assassins who had been created. I've gone through Sirhan's diaries, the diaries he was keeping up to the point he was arrested for the assassination of Senator Robert Kennedy.

B.R.: And he has no idea what happened, does he?

P.L.: He doesn't. I mean, he admits he did it, because he figures, you know, he did it. I mean, if he's arrested for it and he was there, he must have done it. But he has no memory of it. And his diaries are extremely suggestive of someone who's been through a behavior modification program, something like a mind control program. It's fascinating stuff.

B.R.: I read a wonderful book which I've got. I also had the experience of what I guess you could call the International Library Angel suddenly depositing a book at your feet when you're traveling. [*Laughs.*] It was a book by Long John Nebel who was the Art Bell radio host of his day, who operated in the 1950s, who wrote an amazing book about the Control of Candy Jones. You must be familiar with that.

P.L.: Yeah, I do. I'm fascinated by that account as well and I think it's genuine. It's been attacked, of course, by other researchers and authors by saying that Long John Nebel kind of made it up or Candy Jones never went through this.

But if you really go through as I do, which is the thing that I do, is I go through and I try to document what goes on. I met Candy Jones a couple of years before she died. I was actually interviewed by her on radio in New York City.

And from my point of view, what she discusses, especially her trips in Asia and Taiwan, have the absolute ring of truth. I mean, I lived in Asia for a long time. I traveled in those countries. The things that she discusses, I believe, actually did occur. I think that she did not make them up. I can recognize the places she's talking about.

B.R.: I read that book several times and it rang very, very true to me.

P.L.: Yeah. It was not a sensationalistic thing that she was making up. I really do believe what she said happened had happened.

K.C.: So where are you going now with everything? Because you don't really keep your blog up. You had been talking about McCain as a possible mind control victim, and I think there's great evidence to that effect. I'd be interested to hear what you have to say about Obama. I don't know what your current situation is. The Powers That Be, are they aware of you? Have they made your life difficult? Because you seem to be one of the best researchers actually pulling these threads together in one place.

B.R.: And what does this mean for us at the beginning of 2009, looking at the next few years, and what this may mean for this country and the world?

P.L.: Yeah. These are very good questions. I took a little time out for a while to get a graduate degree in religion, and the thesis that I wrote, I published as *Stairway to Heaven*, which came out about a year ago. I have another book on the Freemasons which is coming out in April [2009]. I've kept my hand in all of this, but I've been doing a lot of academic-type work on the one hand, and then a lot of investigative work, on the other.

The political situation... The way I look at it these days, as I mentioned before, is theater. It is basically theater. We are watching a play being acted out in front of us, and we're all willing or unwilling audience members in this play. I think we have to not believe a lot of what we see as being "real." It's a kind of consensus reality. We all kind of agree that certain things are real and certain things are not.

And I always like to talk about the root of the word "*reality*," because the word comes from a very interesting Indo-European root which also gives us "*royal*." It gives us what is real and what is royal. And basically what that means is, to me: "*Whatever the king says is real is real.*"

In other words, there's a kind of agreement that we all enter into, a kind of contract where we agree that certain things are, and certain things are not, *real*. And I think we've come to the point where we have to revisit what we call *real*. We have to revisit reality to a certain extent. We have to come up with a new paradigm, a new way of looking at reality, because it's not working for us, the old way of looking at it. We're too easily manipulated. Our country has made a science of the manipulation of reality since at least the Korean War, if not before.

Communication science, which is being taught in the universities all across the country, came into being as a result of World War Two and psychological warfare studies. I mean, the same guys who created psychological warfare for use during the war were the guys who in the private sector developed programs for teaching advertising, marketing, and communication.

So we are really struggling with psychological warfare being directed against by manipulating our reality.

K.C.: Right. A form of propaganda and mind control in and of itself, just as television becomes in a sense a mind control tool.

P.L.: On a massive, massive scale. I used to live, as I mentioned, in Asia, and we would get CNN out there. I don't want to single out CNN particularly for opprobrium, but they are sort of an international news organization that you can pick up on cable channels all over the world.

There was one particular instance where I'm in Kuala Lumpur and there was a riot going on on CNN, on television, in a restaurant. It was being carried live. And we're looking at the television screen, and we're at the site where this riot is supposed to be taking place. And there's no riot there! [*Kerry laughs.*] We're watching and we're all looking at each other. We're watching the screen and we're saying: "*What is this?*"

It turns out there were three or four people in a corner somewhere and a camera was on them. And the way it looked, it looked as if there were all of these really angry people rioting.

I was getting a phone call from friends of mine saying: "*Go away! Get out! There's a riot taking place. We can see it on television.*" And we're all sitting in the restaurant saying: "*Well, where's the riot?*"

You know, there was no riot. I mean, it was manufactured news, essentially. And if that happened that one time, how many other times has this happened? How much of our news is being manipulated or controlled or created, you know, as we watch it?

K.C.: Right, but as a researcher going into this as deeply as you have, you must be able to look towards the future and come to certain conclusions, and/or think about certain uninvestigated trails to look down.

I am curious: do you think, for example, there are sleeper agents? Because, you know, we keep having these incidents happen and they seem to be evidence of mind control operations in which you have school kids suddenly flipping out, and so on and so forth. Where's it all headed?

P.L.: Well, if we characterize the agents of this madness as individual human beings, we might be missing something darker and something deeper. I believe that there are individual agents, of course, and that's what I investigate. That's what I write about. That's where the evidence leads me.

But sometimes I think that there is something else at work here. I think that there is a kind of level of consciousness that is creating this for us as well, and that we're victims of it because we haven't learned how to fight back. We haven't learned how to take control of our own consciousness. We're essentially allowing others to do that for us.

I think that we have a kind of responsibility, perhaps now more than ever, because the information is available to us, of fighting back by taking control of our own minds, and taking back control of our own consciousness, of trying to deprogram ourselves, if you will, away from what we're being fed on an almost hysterical basis.

I mean, things have ramped up to the point where paranoia, fear, anxiety, stress levels have increased so exponentially, it's as if someone *wants* us to have this collective nervous breakdown. We have to take a stand and fight against it.

I think that if my research has shown nothing [else], it's shown that humans who are involved in this quite often don't really understand it that well themselves. I'm talking about the CIA.

I don't think that the people who ran *MKULTRA* really understood the full ramifications of what they were doing. They had a very narrow focus. They wanted to create deniable assassins, as an example, and that was their focus. They didn't realize the other forces they were unleashing at the time.

And I think that there are paths, there are shamanistic paths, there are paths in the occult that might be actually beneficial for us to investigate to understand how we've been manipulated, how our consciousness has been manipulated, our reality itself has been manipulated. I think we have a chance because there is such an amount of information available.

But we are headed into a very dangerous impasse, a very dangerous place. I agree. But I think that we don't realize how much power we have as individual human beings, or as small groups of individual human beings, to combat this madness. And I think we *can* take back our minds and our lives from these forces, from these sinister forces.

B.R.: Are you able to say anything, do you feel, about the role of the Vatican?

P.L.: Ah… [*Laughs.*] How much time do you have?

B.R.: You know about the work of Eric Phelps and that large body of research that he, among many others, represents. I just wondered if you could pull some of those threads together once again for the benefit of our readers who would like to see as much of a summary of the big picture as you are able to present here.

P.L.: Right. I grew up as a Roman Catholic. I was born into a Catholic family in the pre-Vatican II days. And when Vatican II happened, I was actually kind of disappointed. I didn't like all of the, you know, guitar-playing Masses that were taking place and all this stuff. I felt a little cheated of the mystery, somehow.

But then, as I started to research the Nazi information, that's when Phase One of my disenchantment, or dis-enlightenment, or whatever you want to call it, took place. And that was understanding the degree to which elements within the Vatican had assisted war criminals with hideous records to escape; how they protected them at safe-houses throughout Europe and then in Latin America; how they gave them Vatican passports; how we had the spectacle of Nazi war criminals dressed as priests entering Argentina, entering Brazil, in one case performing a marriage ceremony as a priest. I mean, I can't even imagine what that poor family would have felt had they known that it was a man responsible for the deaths of hundreds if not thousands of people blessing their union as a fake priest. So all of this began to… That was Phase One.

Phase Two was realizing that what we've been told about Christianity itself, particularly about the Catholic Church, is based on so much disinformation and so much manipulation of history and historical facts that we really don't know what the Catholic Church is any more, or what it ever was. We don't know what's going on there.

I mean, the Vatican scandals… The Masonic scandals, the Propaganda Due, the P2 Masonic scandal alone should have alerted people to the degree of perfidy and cupidity that was taking place within the Vatican.

I mean, we had Licio Gelli and Roberto Calvi, all of these characters who were heavily involved in the Vatican and at the same time financing right-wing terror squads, assassination squads, in Europe, in Latin America, working with Francisco Franco – the dictator of Spain for so many years – heavily involved with fascist organizations and operations.

It was mind-numbing, the extent to which this was taking place. So I have a very hard time. I'm thankfully a very lapsed Catholic. You know, I want to stay that way. I can't believe that I would go to the Bishops, Archbishops of the Catholic Church and accept spiritual guidance from people whose morals and ethics I have to question on almost a daily basis.

K.C.: Well, also there's a link between the Vatican, the Illuminati, and the US government, apparently. Can you talk about that a little bit? Because when you're talking about the Nazi influence in America, and you're talking also about The Powers That Be with *Paperclip*, the Ultimate Space Program, and all of the levels at which the Vatican is involved... From what I understand, their secret service was basically the model upon which secret services all over the world have been built.

P.L.: Well, sure. In fact, even the SS... The Nazis emulated the Jesuits. I mean, Himmler wanted to create a Jesuit Order for himself, and that was what the SS was, hence the black uniforms, and the rituals in the churches, and the rituals at night in the forests, and all this other stuff. It was a kind of pagan Jesuit Order that Himmler was trying to create.

I mean, people may have disliked or even hated the Catholic Church or the Vatican, but there was so much of it that they wanted to emulate, that they wanted to duplicate. But the problem is that we have so much information to discuss that it would take hours to get into it. I'll just bring up one or two points that will be enough to scare you, and probably...

I think the place to look in the beginning, if you want to see the connection between the Vatican, Nazis, and even the Illuminati, would be the Knights of Malta and some of the other chivalric orders that the Vatican maintains and supports. I won't go into Opus Dei, which is a whole other kettle of fish by itself. I mean, we're talking about a man, who created that order, who had pro-fascist, pro-Franco sentiments. There's no question about it. And how he could be canonized is absolutely beyond me.

But anyway, look at the Knights of Malta. Look at the connection between the leaders of the CIA, many of whom were Roman Catholics, members of the Knights of Malta or members of one of the other chivalric orders around the Vatican.

When I was growing up in the Bronx in the 1960s, I saw with my own eyes the influence that churches had with intelligence agencies, and intelligence agencies with the churches. I witnessed it as a young man of 18-19 years old, working with a church in the Bronx which was actually a front for intelligence operations.

And that brings us back again to David Ferrie and Jack Martin and the Kennedy assassinations, because I met the Bishops who ordained and consecrated David Ferrie, Jack Martin, all these peripheral figures that you saw in the movie *JFK*, you know, being played by Joe Pesche, being played by Walter Matthau, I think.

These were people who were heavily involved in a church. They were also involved in intelligence activities. They were also involved in anti-Castro Cuban activities and considered to be involved, in one way, shape, or form, with the assassination of a president in Dallas.

So the nexus between religious organizations and intelligence organizations is thick. It's just thick, you know. And like I say, I saw it with my own eyes. I know the church that Ferrie and Martin belonged to in 1968 when Jim Garrison was starting ramping up that investigation into the Kennedy assassination. David Ferrie died mysteriously, but he was a priest and a Bishop with one of these churches. So…

K.C.: Don't you also get into, maybe, what's going on with the agenda, in terms of how this plays out? For example, in the economy of the world going downhill, and the desire for the One World Government. And how there are certain problems being created so that a solution can be created, as you know possibly David Icke's work in that area?

So what I'm wondering is, are you following those threads? Obviously you see the economy going down in America and around the world. There are sacrifices, blood sacrifices. Some of these things, or maybe even all of them, are actually *planned* as some kinds of sacrifices to these hidden, dark entities in order to make certain things happen upon this planet.

P.L.: Well, if we don't characterize the economic situation as a purely economic situation, I think we can see more clearly what's taking place. In a previous era, this might have been a vast military conflict. It might have been a World War Three, or a World War Four. Now we're fighting that same war, but we're using economics to do it. This is a different approach to the same type of general control that's being exerted over the world.

I mean, the whole world cannot go broke. The money is somewhere. That's the funny thing. The humorous part of this thing, if you want to be funny about it… That fact, you know, we're thinking the whole world economy is going down. But basically what happens, especially with capitalism, is somebody gets rich and somebody gets poor. So who's getting rich?

During Watergate we were told to follow the money. And I think if we follow the money today, we can find out who's doing what to whom. We can find out who's actually doing this kind of control.

I've been looking at it. I've been trying. Following the money in today's economy is extremely difficult to do. I think even members of Congress are finding themselves totally unable to explain what's happening. Some of them are not able. Some of them are strictly not willing. But if we can follow the money, if we can start pulling the threads on the money over the last 12 to 18 months, we can probably figure out who's behind this thing.

For me, it's been very difficult to do although I've been trying to cover it. I think the answer is out there. As Fox Mulder used to say, "*The truth is out there.*" But we have to look at the evidence, and the evidence is there. It's just very hard to figure out.

If we're talking about manipulation of the world economy, it's because we're being prepared for something else. Obviously there's an agenda. It's not strictly to make some people rich at the expense of others. That's been going on forever. We don't need a collapse in the world economy to do that. So if a collapse is being engineered, it's to create a circumstance or a set of circumstances conducive to another phase of action which has nothing to do with the economy. As you said, it might be a One World Government – possibly. It might be something more heinous than that.

A collapse of the economy may be a way to keep in place the types of controls that were put into our government during the last eight years. It may be a way of preempting any kind of change that we thought we were voting for – some of us anyway. So there may be a way to…

As 9/11 essentially was a Reichstag fire which gave the president total control of the government, in terms of the Patriot Act and everything else, the collapse in the economy is essentially another 9/11, and it's going to give the government additional powers that it never had.

B.R.: It's just another kind of controlled demolition.

P.L.: Yes. It's a … what's the word I'm looking for … a *consolidation* of all of this. If we put the Patriot Act and some of the other things that took place – the wiretaps, the illegal stuff that's been going on – and we now couple that with government control of banks and corporations, you know, we have *fascism*. Some people are talking about creating socialism or communism here, but fascism is also a wedding between the state and the corporation. It's not just socialism that we're talking about.

The one thing that nobody wants to talk about is the fact that we've been creeping closer and closer to fascism in the last 40 or 50 years. And that scares me, believe it or not, more than socialism does or even communism. What frightens me most is a kind of fascism, an American style of fascism.

K.C.: Well, I mean, this is the premise of Jim Marrs' book, as you know.

P.L.: Yes.

K.C.: And it is a basically a *fait accompli* in the minds of many, even behind the scenes, with Richard Hoagland and his investigation into NASA and the symbolism there, and the *Paperclip* background behind, you know, the space program. So the agenda seems to have been a kind of fascism that stemmed out of World War Two and is being continued today.

But where is that going? Once they have total control, then what? You know, it's almost like they already have total control as it is. One wonders: what next?

And the only thing we've gotten so far in our study of this mystery is the idea of *population elimination*. In other words, they want to eliminate large segments of the population. They haven't been able to do so with other means, with viruses and so on.

In other words, this control you're talking about has to lead to some *thing*, because control is something they have, in a sense, always had. But they're tightening it, and as you say, they're consolidating it. So, with what purpose in mind?

P.L.: Well, that's another good question and it's something, too, that would probably take a long time to try to analyze. I think that "The Powers That Be" are not 100 percent happy yet. They don't really feel they have the kind of control they would like. Part of the reason for that is the explosion of technology, which seems to be getting out of control. You don't notice it perhaps as much in this country as you would overseas where this kind of technology, the Internet in particular, has given people at the grassroots level a voice they never had before.

So the governments in those parts of the world, especially in developing countries, are struggling very hard to control the technology and control access to information.

Right now we are talking over the Internet, and this will be available on the Internet, so people who want to can hear it. But this kind of control eventually will probably have to be extended over what we're doing over the Internet, over the free exchange of information.

I think it's already started, and it's going to continue until there is control over information. And once you control information, you control reality. You control consciousness. Once the independent operators are gone, once they've been closed down, there will only be the party line that's left.

B.R.: That's *1984*, isn't it?

P.L.: Well, it is *1984*. Some people reading this are gonna say to themselves: "*You know, these are the aluminum hat people.*" You know, the tinfoil hats. We're all worried about vast conspiracies taking control.

I want to tell you something, to the readers who maybe think that at times this is out in left field. I was on somewhat friendly terms with a man called Norman Mailer, a famous author, one of America's most famous novelists and journalists and authors, who passed away recently – a man I admired very much. He was kind enough to praise my own work and write a foreword to *Unholy Alliance*. He spoke in my presence about the fact that America was heading towards fascism. Many people of that social setting, other authors, some of them Pulitzer Prize-winning authors, people who are understood to be great thinkers, great members of the *intelligencia*, have all said the same thing to me, or in my presence, that we are heading towards fascism, that America…

According to Norman Mailer, back a couple of years ago, he said America was in what he called a pre-fascist condition, but that we were heading inexorably towards fascism. Other authors since then have said the same thing. So this is not something that only a handful of people on the absolute fringe are feeling. These are things that are being felt on other levels by other people who are not involved in this kind of investigation, people who are not doing this kind of research, people who have just opened their eyes and who've looked around and said: "*My goodness, this is what's going on. We're becoming a fascist country.*"

B.R.: One of the things that confuses people sometimes, as you must be well aware, is the idea that somehow there's a spectrum with socialism on the left and fascism on the right and the two are very different. Actually, they meet in the middle, kind of loop round in a kind of circle, one going to the left and one going to the right. Extreme socialism and extreme fascism are actually very similar.

P.L.: That's the point I was just going to make. To have fascism or to have socialism, you have to have a marriage between the state and business. I mean, that's how it's done.

Either the government owns the means of production as it does in a socialist or a communist country, or the state and the corporations have a working relationship, a nice working relationship, as Eisenhower warned us about when he left office. He talked about the military-industrial complex and how frightened he was that that was happening. That is fascism.

So, does it matter to the average person whether or not the government owns the means of production or the government and the state and the corporations are in bed together? Does it really matter to us on the street?

It's going to be the same effect. We're still going to be controlled. Our economy's going to be controlled. Our freedoms are going to be drastically curtailed. So, in the end, what difference does it make?

I've talked to people about 9/11 a lot. There's been, of course, a lot of discussion about 9/11. And I've always said it was a Reichstag fire. It's what happened in Germany. How Hitler took control of the government was the Reichstag burned down and he blamed the communists for it. And my point was, do we really care who burned down the Reichstag at this point? All we really care about is the fact that it brought Hitler to power.

So, in our case, what did 9/11 do? It pushed all of these heinous attacks on our liberty and our privacy. It pushed them right into the forefront. It made it acceptable. That's what happened. That was the real effect of all of this. We can talk about 9/11 – for instance, we can talk about conspiracies. But let's not lose sight of the fact that what happened, the effect of it, was that we lost more liberty, we lost more privacy.

K.C.: Right. And so then that gets back to the overall agenda.

P.L.: Yes

K.C.: And it's not a conspiracy theory. It's a conspiracy fact when you look at all the evidence. And what's happening is that this particular agenda is being rolled out.

And, of course, it's very heartening that you do talk about how consciousness, and the role of consciousness, was getting out of the hands of the people in *MKULTRA*, such that people like Gottlieb himself, who was certainly one of the masterminds behind all of that, goes on his own sojourn to India, looking for some kind of spiritual way out, I think, of the responsibility for which he… You know, it's basically like walking around in some kind of living hell, I'm sure, being inside that guy's head.

And so, in essence, all of this is playing out in the microcosm around the globe, not just America, because I see it in many countries. In fact,

England has the best surveillance system on the streets, cameras, etcetera. So what's happening is, on some level it seems to be manifesting in America sort of in a more overt way. But in a covert way, it's actually existed in small countries, under despots that were financed by the CIA, and then across the globe, masterminding the governments behind countries like Switzerland, and so on.

P.L.: Well, what's very amusing to me in a sardonic sort of way is the fact that in the United States, if you talk about conspiracies, you're pooh-poohed. You're shot down. It's considered, you know, paranoid fantasy. And yet we recognize without hesitation the fact that conspiracies like this exist in every other country on the planet. Right? So when Benazir Bhutto, the former prime minister of Pakistan, was gunned down last year in Pakistan, everyone said of course it was a conspiracy. There were elements of the Pakistani secret police involved. Al Quaeda may be involved, or the Taliban, or who knows what. But automatically it was a conspiracy.

However, according to mainstream historians, not a single person assassinated in this country has ever been assassinated by a conspiracy! [*Laughs.*] No conspiracy. Nothing to see here. Move along. Right? We have this idea somehow that the US is immune to these events.

And yet we overthrow dictators in foreign countries. We've overthrown and committed assassinations in Guatemala, in Iran back in the days of the Shah. We overthrew the government of Allende in Chile. We put Pinochet in power. All of these things we do on a regular basis and we've done it for years and years and years. And yet somehow it doesn't take place inside the United States. Why is that? Why is it so impossible to believe?

K.C.: Right. And I think, though, nowadays it's a lot easier to sort of get people to, not so much believe, but really understand the roots of conspiracy. And ever since the death of Kennedy, I think that America's eyes have slowly been opened along those lines, at least many. Although certainly 9/11, you still get people not able to accept the possibility that a conspiracy took place there. So, again, I guess we've gone full circle with you. In many ways we're going over some material here that is just … the roots are everywhere. The conspiracies, if you will, are everywhere.

It's very heartening to know that you are behind the wheel, investigating all of this and documenting it and pulling as many threads together as you are. I encourage people to follow your work. I certainly want to read a lot more that you've written.

P.L.: Where I'm going now? I'm still in the midst of all of this, you know? I'm still in the midst of researching. I don't know what my next book will be. As I had mentioned, I have a book on Freemasons coming out in April, which is kind of a look at the connection between the Masonic society and the Mormons, and some of the occultism that was taking place in our country before, during, and after the revolution, the American Revolution. So I look at the connections that were there. It's kind of a general look at Freemasonry. I'm not a Freemason myself, of course. That's coming out in April.

Stairway to Heaven was really more about Kabbalah and Chinese alchemy and that sort of thing, a very spiritually oriented book trying to understand some of the implications of some of the ancient writings.

So, where I'm going to go from here? I'm constantly collecting information. I'm constantly building up files of data, trying to see more connections, and I'm sure I'll have something like this to share with you soon.

K.C.: That's fabulous. One thing I do want to ask you, the book you were talking about that you investigated the occult quite deeply...

P.L.: I was involved with it. Yeah. *The Necronomicon*. Of course. I mean, I made no secret of that. I've done some interviews based on that. That was an occult work that, I think today it's one of the critical texts, probably, of the mid-20th century on occultism. It's been reviled by a lot of people. People claim it's a hoax. Other people say it's a very terrible book, or it's a very powerful work. I look at it as the survival of an old Middle Eastern occult practice which involved a process of initiations, going through a series of "gates," gaining greater and greater illumination or enlightenment at each time, each passing of the "gate." It's an interesting book, and the events around it were interesting as well.

K.C.: Well, thank you, Peter. This has been fascinating. We're both really very interested in what you're gonna be doing in the future, as well as to get into your work after this conversation. And thank you for taking the time today to talk to us.

P.L.: It was my pleasure. Thank you very much.

Audio interview recorded on February 12, 2009.
Published in issue 3 of The Dot Connector magazine (May-June 2009).

Were Humans Created as Slaves?

Michael Tellinger

In an age where technology has allowed us to expect instant reward and provides us with immediate solutions, humankind seems to have all the answers. Our confidence as a species is higher than ever before and the knowledge of the universe we live in is expanding faster than most people can keep up with. We can compute and calculate the landing of a small probe on a planet 100 million miles away; we know what the atmosphere on Jupiter consists of; we can regenerate new organs in our bodies and genetic engineers can create new life in any shape or size they want to. There are, however, three fundamental questions that we have not been able to answer. Who are we? How did we get here? And, why are we here?

Ever since I first became interested in genetics, it has always intrigued me that such an important part of our anatomy, the genome, a molecular structure so refined, should have been created incomplete. Actually, the truth is that the genome was created in abundance, with large parts of the structure that are not being used at all. It is as if the inactive parts of the genome are waiting for some extrinsic factor to switch them on. The question begs, which unimaginable characteristics or super abilities are the dormant parts of the genome not controlling? What human abilities are they hiding? And how has this affected our evolution as a species?

The genome is just another name for the full complement of genes and DNA contained by an individual. In humans, the genome consists of 23 pairs of chromosomes which contain the entire genetic programme for that specific individual and is located in the nucleus of every cell in our bodies. This genetic programme controls all the information that allows us to grow and function. Our genome is unique for every individual and every species. When we are born, we are blissfully unaware of what awaits us. There might be seven ages of man, but it all ends up woven together into a long reality performance directed by some invisible force. We are all given some 70 years to do our performance here on Earth, on average; the rest is up to each one of us. Enter stage left ... exit stage right. The only certainty we have at present is that we will exit. What are you going to do with your 70 years? What is the purpose of this journey, this play of life that we all participate in? Will you use this time creatively, make a contribution to the global community of beings, or will you be a mere spectator, a usurper of facilities before you exit stage right?

Despite the 6.5 billion people who populate the Earth, the human race is a rather fragile and primitive species. No matter how intelligent and smart we think we are, we constantly display signs of basic animal behaviour that can lead to the decimation of our kind in the blink of an eye. We have waged war on our fellow man throughout history and continue to do so into the 21st century. There always seems to be a moral high ground or justification for our action. From Cain and Abel to George W. Bush, it has always been the strong and powerful who oppress and wipe out the weak. The old testament of the Bible is not a pretty tale of compassion and forgiveness. In fact, quite the opposite. It talks about an eye for an eye; wiping out man, woman, child and beast in the name of god; and often mentions the enemy by name, personifying them as the 'bad' guys or disciples of the devil. It seems that god has been taking sides from the very beginning. He had his favourites, and then there were 'the others.' I always felt that the God I have been told about should be more impartial and loving.

The Bible is filled with prophets and other individuals who for thousands of years had a direct link to god and who on a regular basis received instructions from god to do certain things. When reading the Bible, it is not only deemed normal, but it is expected of us to take for granted and to believe that a number of 'chosen' people received such regular instructions from god. Not only did they receive clear instructions and warnings, they received physical instructions in the form of the Ten Commandments and rewards of a material kind, like land or cattle. But the most impressive interactions between god and man were the many visitations god made in person to various individuals. If he could not make it in person, he would send 'angels' to deal with whatever situation needed to be dealt with. The divine beings would share ideas, share wine and bread, and inevitably god would instruct the person to perform certain tasks. All of these individuals seem to have been men. And all of the people who contributed to the scriptures of the Bible were also all men. If 'He' created us all equal, did god have a problem with the credibility of women? Or was god just the personification of a male dominated society? The simple historic fact remains – that god actually physically interacted with man. Today such claims of a physical interaction with God would draw strong criticism and ridicule. Why is that? Is it perhaps that such events in prehistory cannot affect us here today? We seem to accept it when it happened in ancient history, almost reduced to some fantastic fairy tale of our struggle for freedom. Or is it simply because we are too scared to analyse the facts for fear of victimisation by placing such arguments in the public domain? These questions have troubled me for most of my life.

And who, and when, decided that the Bible had reached its conclusion? That it was now enough, it is now the end, and the final chapter must be written! Obviously, this was another man inspired by God and dictated to by the Holy Spirit! Surely the quest for truth and salvation continues? Surely the atrocities on Earth have not abated; surely the people of the Earth need ongoing guidance and instructions from God on how to deal with modern day mayhem and crime; how to respond to dictators; how to survive colonisation, racism, invasions and other inventions of 'evil' minds. Our capacity for cruelty as a species has reached unbearable proportions. We make rules as civilised beings, only to be abused and used against us by less civilised individuals with a good knowledge of the legal system. Those who preach peace and love and turning the other cheek have become the weakened victims of their own philosophy.

Now, more than ever, people need salvation. They need something real to believe in and to hold onto in times when all hope seems to have vanished. So why are the scriptures not ongoing? Why is God not dictating more wisdom through one of his prophets? Or many of his prophets? Some say He is. Many claim they are in contact with God on a regular basis. Many convey God's messages in packed churches and other places of worship. How does the global community respond to individuals who make fantastic claims of miracles, and hearing God's voice, and having the answer? Well, in many cases these modern prophets rise to a cult status with a blind following of disciples who will respond to every command, while in other cases they are reduced to cranks with a loose screw.

So, how should a judge in the 21st century respond to a guy who tied up his ten-year-old daughter to a table in the back yard, and who was caught by police in the process of stabbing her to death or slitting her throat? If he claims that God had instructed him to sacrifice her to prove his obedience to the all mighty lord, should such a character be seen as an example of a modern faithful or a psychopath? Yet we look at Abraham as a faithful man of God with strong principles and a leader of men because he obeyed god's instructions to 'kill' his own son. The Bible, however, calls it 'sacrifice'. Would we see it as such if it happened today in a wealthy suburb of Johannesburg or Paris?

It is truly a confusing state of religious activity out there. Thousands of religions, all of them man-made, all claiming that they have the answer. Only 'their' followers will be saved by the maker and bask in the pleasures of paradise. It seems that the more money they have, the more power they wield and the closer to God's ear they can get.

And so the religious argument begins, and we clearly display the primitive side of our low evolutionary state. Are these the primitive characteristics which could be controlled by the inactive genes? We look at the past great civilisations and somehow feel superior. The fact that we cannot explain many things from prehistory is quickly discarded as *"who cares about the Egyptians ... they're all dead"*. In the light of all our achievements and scientific discoveries, the more we evolve, the stronger the religious dogma becomes. It seems that the religious dogma, which could also be called fanaticism in this case, is directly linked to money. The wealthier a nation, the more they can enforce their particular religious views on others. The USA may claim that they are a 'free' society in all respects, but that is mainly because they feel a sense of comfort among their 96% Christian community. It is safe for them to allow the minority 'rogue' religions to waste their time on their own meaningless salvation.

But then we start to look at who we really are, and the road we have travelled as a species on this planet, only to realise that our presence here does not even equate to the 'tip of the iceberg'. We marvel at dinosaur fossils and talk about what it must have been like here on Earth when dinosaurs roamed. We throw around numbers like '60 million years', when they were extinct; '200 million years' when T-Rex caused havoc, and '400 million years' ago really makes us gasp at the fossils of insects in the museums. Then we start comparing the timescale to famous events in our own frame of reference. The First World War 100 years ago; Leonardo da Vinci 500 years ago; the Vikings some 1,200 years ago; Mohammed some 1,400 years ago; Jesus 2,000 years ago; the pyramids 4,000 years ago; the last ice age some 13,000 years ago; by then most of us run out of reference points.

And then one day something miraculous happens. We lift our eyes up at the night sky filled with billions of stars and we try to imagine infinity. Someone points out Mars and Jupiter. And then you look through a telescope and for the first time you see Saturn with its rings and even several of its moons, and suddenly the reality of it all changes somewhat. It all becomes a little bit bigger. You look at Alpha Centauri and realise that the light from the closest star to us takes five years to reach us, travelling at 300,000 km per second. You go to a lecture by an astronomer and see pictures of galaxies so far away it is impossible to imagine the distance. Galaxies a billion light years away. Super-cluster galaxies five billion light years away; ultra hot quasars some 12 billion light years away right at the edge of the known universe, and then ... some 13.8 billion light years away... just blackness. Nothing. You sit in silent contemplation as you try to digest the reality of what you have just witnessed. You have just looked beyond the edge of the known universe, where nothing exists.

But when you wake up in the morning and you try to explain your epiphany to a group of close friends, they share your excitement for exactly 15 seconds before one of them pronounces, *"Hey, did you guys check that lekker (nice) movie on TV last night?"*

With all the valiant attempts and sometimes remarkable discoveries by archaeologists, we still cannot pinpoint the origin of humankind. Oh, scores of scientist will argue and give you all kinds of evidence and proof, only to be rewritten by some new scientist five years from now. It is all calculated speculation presented to us either as scientific hypotheses or religious dogma. But in reality, all it ends up being, is more manipulation of the pieces of the Great Human Puzzle. We cannot tell when civilised man first walked the Earth and we cannot tell when man was created, or how man evolved, with a definite level of certainty.

Let's face it, the past two centuries have led to amazing discoveries of ancient civilisations, lost cities and a closer understanding of the people who developed these ancient cultures. Cultures that displayed remarkable knowledge and understanding of science and the cosmos. It has taken us decades to decipher the various texts or styles of writing by the many extinct cultures. With all our knowledge and sophistication, we have not deciphered the Balkan-Danube script and the Indus Script to date. The diversity of these ancient civilisations, from the ancient Chinese, various cultures of the Americas, the hieroglyphs of the Egyptians, to the cuneiform scriptures of the Sumerians, the lost cities of Asia, have baffled historians and archaeologists alike. It has taken us by complete surprise to discover ancient libraries, such as the library of King Ashurbanipal at Nineveh, with around 30,000 cuneiform clay tablets of scriptures that point to great knowledge by lost civilisations.

It is curious to discover the extended knowledge of astronomers as early as six thousand years ago with detailed information of our own solar system, describing it in great detail. We read about ancient gods who roamed and ruled the Earth, in chariots that flew in from the stars, and conflicts and betrayal between these ancient gods. We read about brave men who achieved great things in the distant past and wisdom which was imparted to man by the many gods who came from the stars. The ability to extract precious metals from ore in the ground, while the production of gold, copper, tin and bronze as early as nine thousand years ago points to clear understanding of metallurgical procedure. The ancient ruins of the Americas with visible extraction and mining activity explain why there was an unimaginable wealth of gold in this part of the world long before Columbus, Cortes or the other savages who set foot there only a few hundred years ago. The further inexplicable evidence of ore mining in southern Africa as far back as 100,000 years ago is simply too much for even the bravest of archaeologists to accept.

The knowledge of medical procedure and genetic manipulation, the creation of the 'Adamu' and a new species, is clearly documented in ancient tablets which have only recently been understood by so-called intelligent man. The power of wireless communication and geophysical knowledge to anticipate natural disaster; all this wealth of information stares us bluntly in the face. And yet, we cannot come to terms with the fact that we may not be the pinnacle of intelligence that has inhabited the planet. Since the rapid evolution of the computer, our ability to document and match this ancient wisdom has enabled us to understand it more clearly. But what do we do with all this information when standing face-to-face with incredible tales from prehistory? We have two choices. Either we believe that it has been left for future civilisations to use and build upon, or we discard it as hallucinogenic garbage by some primitive idiots from a stone age, not worthy of our attention.

But the fact that only 500 years ago men were burnt at the stake for suggesting that Earth was not the centre of the universe; the human body was a mysterious vessel that was studied and dissected by daring scientists risking their lives in the early hours of the morning; that we only discovered the last three planets in our solar system in the past 200 years – are clear indications that we are not the super race.

We are the sub-species. Our arrogance is our weakness, and our ignorance a congenital disease that will eventually destroy us. The dogma has consumed us and the fear controls us. But why are we so blind to the facts and evidence that surround us? Why are we so obsessed with popular religions that mostly bow to a god who uses retribution and punishment as a form of control? If we all come from the same maker, we should all have the same set of rules on how to obey that maker, but this is clearly not the case. Religious conflict has torn our history apart for millennia and still hangs over our heads into the 21st century like a cancer waiting to devour us. ... Our disorder is the direct result of our bastard race status, with unpredictable animal behaviour lurking in our manipulated double helix DNA. Our intelligence has been suppressed, our knowledge has been erased, our lifespan has been genetically shortened and our memory has been removed. We are an inferior, genetically cloned mutation of the great civilisations of the past, left behind to pick up the pieces, or to put together the pieces of the Great Human Puzzle.

We have made remarkable progress in the field of genetic engineering, but just because we have been able to 'map' the genome does not mean we know everything about it. On the contrary. The more we learn about the genome, the more we marvel at its complexity. We seem to understand the basic principle of the double helix, but we are far from understanding all its functions. What we are especially perplexed by, are the large sections that seem to be 'switched off.' Yes, it is curious to learn that there are large parts of the genome which are not active. Ever since I first became interested in the study of the genome, I have been fascinated by the strange phenomenon, that such a masterful part of our anatomy, a molecular structure so refined, should have been created incomplete. That kind of discovery flies directly in the face of all evolutionary processes. But the real truth is that the genome was created in abundance, with far more DNA in our cells than we need for our primitive form. It is as if the inactive parts of the genome are waiting for some extrinsic factor to switch them on.

This begs the question. If the genome controls all our characteristics and bodily functions, then what is it that is not controlled by the inactive parts of the genome? I firmly believe that this is the ultimate question of humanity. What inert secret powers are being locked up behind the inactive parts of our genetic structure?

Let's take a quick look at the history of genetic discovery. While there is clear evidence of prehistoric genetic activity and manipulation dating back to some 250,000 years ago, modern man has only rediscovered the genome in the 1950s. In 1866, Gregor Mendel published the results of his investigations of the inheritance of 'factors' in pea plants, but it was only in the 1950s that the chemical structure of the DNA was rediscovered by modern scientists. They finally had a name for it, *deoxyribonucleic acid.* The people involved in this breakthrough were Maurice Wilkins, Rosalind Franklin, Francis H. C. Crick and James D. Watson. With this discovery they started a whole new branch of science, namely molecular biology. In the same decade, Watson and Crick made history when they made the first model of the DNA molecule, showing its twisted double helix structure, and proved that genes determine heredity. In 1957, Arthur Kornberg produced DNA in a test tube. 1963 saw F. Sanger develop the sequencing procedure for proteins. By 1966, a real breakthrough was made when the genetic code was discovered. Scientists were now able to predict characteristics by studying DNA. This very quickly evolved into genetic engineering and genetic counselling.

In 1972, Paul Berg produced the first recombinant DNA molecule, and in 1983, Barbara McClintock was awarded the Nobel Prize for her discovery that genes are able to change position on chromosomes. In the late 1980s, an international team of scientists began the tedious and demanding task of mapping the human genome, and the first crime conviction based on DNA fingerprinting, in Portland, Oregon, took place. By 1990, gene therapy was used on patients for the first time. In 1993, Dr. Kary Mullis discovered the PCR procedure, for which he was awarded the Nobel Prize. In 1994, the FDA approved the first genetically engineered food. These were Flavr Savr tomatoes engineered for better flavour and shelf life.

By 1995, criminal DNA forensics made headlines in the O. J. Simpson trial. In 1997, Dolly the Sheep was cloned as the first adult animal clone. 1998 saw the senate inquiry into the Clinton/Lewinsky scandal based largely on DNA evidence, and in the year 2000, J. Craig Venter, along with

Francis Collins, jointly announced the completion of the mapping and sequencing of the entire human genome. This was a major achievement that took almost 10 years less than originally expected. In 2003, Craig Venter launched a global expedition to obtain and study microbes from environments ranging from the world's oceans to urban centres. This mission will yield a definitive insight into genes that make up the vast realm of microbial life. And now the true genetic era is upon us. The first pet cloning company opened their doors for business in the USA in 2004. In essence, we have become the creators of species. And so we have become 'god' to those species we create.

The more we discover in the Cradle of Humankind in South Africa, the more we can genetically link the various peoples of the world to half a dozen original individuals in southern Africa; the more evidence we get from female mitochondrial DNA that the first human was born around 250,000 years ago, the more the pieces of the puzzle seem to fit. In this book [see footnote on page 72] we will explore written evidence that places such a group of primordial humans in southern Africa some 200,000 years ago, at about the time when the Adam was supposed to have been created. When I first started placing these pieces together, I was doubtful that something so fantastic could be a possibility. But if you allow yourself the freedom of thought and possibility, you will discover an incredible story with a clear vision of the past, and you will begin to unravel the great steps of humanity that brought us here.

This brings us to the age-old question. "*Who are we ... and why are we here?*" No, it is not really a 'hey-shoo-wow' kind of question, it is possibly one of the most complex riddles of our species, which deserves a fresh new look and possibly a slightly less conventional approach if we want to reach new and refreshing answers. But then we must be prepared to face answers we may not have expected. This is what I intend to share with you in this book. What may at first seem like a horror story, will turn out to be the most liberating experience that brought me much closer to God than I ever imagined possible. Once again I have to draw your attention to the difference between God, the creator of the universe and all things in it, and 'god' one of many deities who walked the Earth over millennia, wielding power, knowledge and technology with which they ruled over humanity.

There is good news for those who believe in the 'creation' theory, that man was created by God and given certain rules to live by. Those who believe in the evolutionary theory have a few surprises to face. Evidence that has been uncovered and contained in the many Sumerian tablets, suggests that the 'Adamu' was created here on Earth in the image of his 'maker.' But who created Adam, and when, will reveal that he was created by an advanced species of deities for a specific purpose here on Earth some 200,000 to 250,000 years ago. We further learn from the tablets that Adam was created from the genetic pool of the advanced species of humans on Earth and a lesser evolved hominid that roamed in southern Africa. But who were these 'advanced humans' and where did they appear from? And why is there no fossil evidence of their existence?

I must once again remind you of the dilemma we face when we contemplate such outlandish theories, as most, if not all of our facts come from prehistoric clay tablets that have been deciphered over the last 50 years of the 20th century. We have to make a personal choice, whether we believe that what was written in these tablets is close enough to the truth, or whether it is merely some hallucinogenic garbage from a time when people's minds did not function properly. I, for one, have made my decision to take at face value what has been written. I cannot imagine for one minute that thousands of people spent millions of man-hours painstakingly creating these tablets, if their contents were less than relevant. I am convinced that they had better things to do than trying to confuse future generations about our origins. After all, we have not really changed that much; we also want to leave evidence of our intellect and achievements, not only for future generations but also for other advanced species in the vastness of the universe. Why else would we send space probes filled with human paraphernalia, videos, compact discs, books, photographs, TV shows and other symbols of our existence into space? At the back of our minds and against the belief of millions, there is the faint hope that there may be advanced life somewhere in the universe. If there is, we hope to dazzle it with our brilliance or disappoint them with our ignorance, all depending on how evolved they may be by the time they accidentally recover our earthly 'space ark.'

It has always amazed me how many people show a complete disregard for history. To many … the past simply does not matter. But if we don't know who we are and where we come from, how can we begin to understand where we might be going, on our path of progress and evolution?

So we toil away and dream of better days. We close ourselves in cocoons of comfort, position our blinkers squarely on our heads and try not to step too far out of the lane of conformity. We believe that if we work hard or if we work smart we will achieve some sort of reward at the end of all of this. We take out insurance policies to reward our offspring and retirement annuities to cruise through the last few years of our own time on this planet. We keep procreating as if we were programmed to do so. It seems to be a natural step in our maturing process. And unbeknown to us, it is most likely driven by our genome in an attempt to continue surviving while our DNA evolves towards its own completion. On this path of evolution, it unlocks the secret parts, which have been switched off by some alchemist in our distant past. We pray for health, wealth and happiness. Some dream of eternal life and many pray for salvation, but deep inside there seems to bubble the burning desire to find answers to the great human question… *"Who am I, and why am I here?"*

History gives us many clues about who we may be, and by stringing together the events and behavioural patterns of humans in the past, history does give us some clues as to where we are heading. Whether we will survive to get there is another question all together. History does not, however, always clearly answer the question of who we are and where we come from. Historians, archaeologists and anthropologists have painted a very predictable past for us. Aside from the arguments between creationists and evolutionists, the story of humanity and humankind has become an almost pretty fairy tale, and most humans do not want their fairy tale disrupted. Humanity rose from the ashes against all odds; we survived and grew in numbers while spreading over the Earth. We discovered fire, iron, bronze, silver and gold. We learnt new skills, adopted farming instead of roaming, buried our dead, learnt to live in structured communities, learnt to write and built cities to protect us from the bad guys. Then we learnt to trade, found democracy, discovered mechanisation, discovered technology, reached for the stars, and all the time we have been killing each other in the name of our god, our king, or for some other perfectly justifiable reason.

It is truly a miracle that we have survived all this. It is clear that, somewhere in our DNA, there is a violent gene that plays a prominent role in human behaviour. This is a great story, but it only really deals with the past 6,000 years or so. Prior to this it gets very murky, and somehow the timing does not seem to fit. The question of the missing link is now more relevant than ever before. Our genome has certainly evolved to the point where we can at least ponder these questions and challenge some of the obvious conventions. But this evolution seems to be more spiritual or mental. Physical evolution is debatable. If we have not really evolved physically in the past 6,000 years since the Egyptians and Sumerians, why should we believe that we underwent some dramatic evolution the previous 6,000 years… or the 10,000 years before that? It appears that our genome has been evolving around the mental parts only. As if we had some catching up to do mentally. This kind of genetic imbalance seems to point to some sort of tampering in the ancient past.

Survival of the fittest has been embraced as one of the pivotal evolutionary arguments. Terms like 'natural selection' have been introduced and presented with dramatic evidence. It may have been the case in the protozoa, the dinosaurs or the horse, but there seem to be serious gaps in the prehistoric evolutionary patterns of humans. Dramatic jumps in evolution, which will form part of my argument, point to the horrible truth that we are a *slave species*, purposefully created to perform a mundane function here on this Earth. It is for us to collect the clues and string them together to formulate a sensible answer.

Some will not find any sense in my logic, but some will hopefully become more tolerant of the unknown and the forbidden questions of the past. One of the highest hurdles to cross will be the real possibility that we might have to come to terms with two gods. One with a capital 'G', and the other with a small 'g'. The difference between the two should be obvious, and our prehistory seems to be filled with events which tend to favour the needs and whims of the latter. Have we been conned since the beginning to believe that some form of advanced deity was actually God? If so, did he give us the rules, the scriptures, and the punishment? Was it in his image that we were created? There is an overwhelming amount of written evidence pointing to this conclusion. Do we start to take this ancient knowledge more seriously, giving it the respect it deserves, or do we respond to our overwhelming enslavement by dogma, and discard all this ancient knowledge? I will leave it up to you to draw your own conclusions.

Excerpt from the book Slave Species of god *(2005,* ISBN: *1920070133).*
Published in issue 5 of The Dot Connector magazine (September-October 2009).

Beyond Exopolitics

A personocratic view of the extraterrestrial phenomena

Mado

Exopolitics study the relationship between human beings and extraterrestrials (ET) or other non-human intelligent beings. It is a subject of prime importance since the origin of humanity; its religions, history, technology, politics and future cannot be clearly understood without first considering exopolitics. Defining the scope of the phenomenon is difficult since, for in the past sixty years, the media has imprisoned the subject within walls of ridicule.

Meanwhile, the government has kept anything that was remotely related to exopolitics hidden under a thick veil of secrecy

A few numbers will help us realize the amplitude of the phenomenon. USA seems to be the country most affected by UFO sightings. According to ICAR (International Community for Alien Research), 50 percent of US citizens believe that Earth has been and is still visited by ET, 15 percent have seen UFO from close enough to be able to give construction details, and 2 percent (5 millions!) were probably abducted by ET. The same scenario repeats itself in all countries, usually with lower ratios. However, everywhere in the world, almost 100 percent of the population believe that their government has been lying about the subject. What information is being kept away from us under this insidious concealment and disinformation?

Any person willing to study exopolitics open-mindedly will quickly discover an incredible amount of facts – documents, witnesses, photographs, videos, skeletons, architecture, paintings, technologies, and so on – that cannot be explained otherwise. The incredible performances of UFO have often taken the breath away from military and civilian pilots, astronauts, and engineers. These UFO appear and disappear out of nowhere, travel at incredible speeds and make 90 degree angles without slowing down, an impossible feat according to the law of inertia. One cannot study the following phenomena without considering a possible extraterrestrial origin: crop circles, cattle mutilations, certain human implants, some human abductions during which ET and human beings went directly through walls or travelled outside of the usual space and time limits.

Since the amount of undeniable proof has been steadily increasing, why do most governments, including USA's, still refuse to publicly acknowledge the UFO-ET phenomenon? Why do other governments (France, Great Britain, Canada, Mexico, Brazil and Denmark) open up only a portion of their previously "cleansed" files? When one digs deeper, the reason becomes obvious. Most of the military and paramilitary groups involved in exopolitics have been using threats, torture, drugs (traffic and experimentation), mind control, abductions, money laundering and murder to keep the truth from coming out. The stories published by whistleblowers have been purposefully riddled with disinformation to such an extent that it is presently impossible to study exopolitics without falling into pits filled with lies and deceit.

Meanwhile, leisure media (movies, TV series, video games) and New Age spirituality manipulate our exopolitical belief system with breathtaking ability. In some scenarios, good ET will come and save us when things start to heat up on Earth. In other scenarios, bad ET are ready to invade us, or have been deviously controlling us for millennia. Good or bad, extraterrestrials are always presented as being far more intelligent, knowledgeable and powerful than humans. Humanity remains the poor victim who is forever searching for a culprit to point at and a saviour to pray to. For some, the future world government will save them from an invasion of cruel and scheming ET. For others, wise and saintly ET will insure that the scheming secret elite in charge of the military-industrial-extraterrestrial complex will not jeopardize human survival on our planet.

It is time to examine the exopolitical scene with a *personocratic*[1] vision. Human beings have never been victims but creators. As long as a human being remains unconscious of her creative nature, she cannot climb out of the hell-on-earth she has created. To raise her consciousness, she absolutely needs to understand the exopolitical scene, as it touches upon all aspects of her daily life.

Exopolitics and History

Many artefacts prove that extremely advanced civilizations existed on Earth thousands of years ago, although we cannot be sure that they were human-made. Let us examine a few examples. Ancient submerged cities were found near Bimini and Yonaguni that are possibly tens of thousands of years old. Some ancient architectural feats would be very difficult, if not impossible, to imitate with modern technology, due to their weight or complexity: cromlechs (Stonehenge), sculptures (Easter Island), pyramids (Egyptian, Mayan).

Let us mention old castle walls that were probably vitrified because of a nuclear explosion (Scotland), ancient and extremely precise maps (Piri Reis, 1513), dinosaurs killed by lasers, a 500,000 year old battery, geoglyphs such as the Nazca lines in Peru, and a thousand other proofs. It quickly becomes obvious that ancient and extremely advanced civilizations – human or/and non-human – preceded our own.

To discover the identity of our pre-modern era builders and inventors, we must leaf through the pages of various religious texts: Bible, Koran, Torah, Vedas. These are filled with stories of UFO, which are described as burning bushes, chariots of fire, wheels of light, *vimanas*. Their pilots are portrayed as angels coming down from heaven or demons suddenly springing up from the fires of hell. Several medieval paintings show UFO, some with ET on board. It seems obvious that at least some of the "gods" of old and other mythical characters who have inspired religions and spiritualities were extraterrestrial in origin.

Extraterrestrials Created Human Beings

Sumerian tablets and biblical accounts describe the creation of human beings by "creator gods" bearing names such as Annunaki (Sumerian) or Elohim (Hebrew). According to these texts and many others, we can conclude that a human being is a genetically modified organism (GMO), probably made up of the genes of a terrestrial hominid, *Homo erectus*, to which were added gene segments of several extraterrestrial species: reptilians (demons), Aryan-types (angels) and others. Alex Collier mentions 22 different genomes used to create the human DNA. By using different combinations, our ET "creator gods" were able to invent several human races on Earth. Some disappeared (Neanderthal), possibly decimated by their creators who wished to favour the races that best suited their needs. Among them were also found giant races – Nephilim, Rephaim, Anakim. These are mentioned in the Bible and their skeletons have been found in many places on the planet (China, USA, India). Our "divine" geneticists invented the *Homo sapiens* GMO for two reasons. First, they were to be used as slaves in mines, because ET workers were ill-adapted to life on Earth. Secondly, human beings were meant to serve as cattle [2] for their masters, who needed food that was adapted to their genetic makeup in Earth's difficult environment.

These genetic experiments probably took place about 200,000 years ago, with several subsequent improvements. An extremely rapid evolution followed, as human civilisations bloomed and collapsed in succession. Hunter-gatherers became farmers and small settlements blossomed into various large cities in Sumer, Egypt, India and Mesoamerica. Some of the oldest official historical records date back 5000 years and demonstrate the presence of an advanced Sumerian civilisation in such fields as religion, architecture, art, politics, law, money and education. Domesticated plants and animals were surely developed through advanced genetic manipulations by our extraterrestrial geneticists, in order to sustain their agricultural needs on Earth and that of their human slaves.

All ancient human civilisations on Earth mention tall and powerful creator gods, often with partially animal bodies that are pictured as insect-like, reptilian, bird-like or mammalian. Some of these are represented in ancient Egyptian culture. Many were described as large snakes, often with legs and sometimes wings, corroborating the legends about dragons that are found on all continents. Did human beings kill off all the descendants of these extraterrestrial geneticists, like St. George did to his mythical dragon? Human beings may have become violent and smart enough that our extraterrestrial geneticists decided to leave the planet or remain in partial hiding in out-of-reach places, usually underground. Is this the source of legends mentioning demons living in a mysterious underground hell?

Different Types of Intelligent Beings

Several types of intelligent non-human beings (INHB) can be encountered on Earth. According to whistleblower Clifford Stone, 57 different species are known by the US Army. Before the creation of human beings, some intelligent non-human beings lived on Earth or visited our planet on a regular basis. To help our understanding of the phenomenon, it is easier to divide these various intelligent non-human beings into four groups, according to their origin and our capacity to perceive them. For a quick overview, check the square on the right.

TYPES OF INTELLIGENT BEINGS
(from a human perspective)

1 – human beings (HB);
2 – intelligent non-human beings (INHB):
  a) extraterrestrials (ET),
  b) intraterrestrials (IT),
  c) extrasensorials (ES),
  d) hybrid human beings (HHB).

The 57 species mentioned earlier belong to two groups of intelligent non-human beings: extraterrestrials (ET) and intraterrestrials (IT). The most common category is the typical ***extraterrestrial*** travelling inside various types of UFO and coming from elsewhere. All the ET who are able to reach our planet can manipulate the space-time continuum and get to or leave Earth very quickly. They may arrive from another planet in our solar system (Venus, Mars), a different star system within our galaxy (Vega, Rigel), or a distant galaxy (Andromeda, Sombrero).

The second category is made up of ***intraterrestrials*** (IT). These live on Earth, usually underground or underwater. Some inhabit huge caves (100 to 200 miles deep) while others live underneath army bases where they work with humans on secret projects (Los Alamos, Dulce). Several species of intraterrestrials travel with UFO. A few persons (Amiral Byrd, Olaf Jansen, modern pilots) mention that the Earth is hollow and inhabited by various races of IT living in large, technologically advanced cities. The Earth crust is approximately 821 miles thick and there are huge openings at both poles.

Much more mysterious, the third category of intelligent non-human beings represents what I have chosen to call ***extrasensorials*** (ES). The main problem comes from the fact that human beings use five very limited senses – sight, hearing, taste, smell and touch – that give them access to about 0.1 percent of their environment, according to physicist Giuliana Conforto. Consequently, many types of intelligent non-human beings are difficult to identify and contact unless one has extrasensory abilities. Certain drugs, technologies, dowsing, sacred geometry and magical ceremonies allow us to perceive their presence. These are beings from the supraphysical, vital (emotional, astral) or mental (spiritual) realms. Some can modify their appearance and pretend to be ET, IT, demons, angels, saints or a dead parent in order to better manipulate us. Power-hungry extrasensorials can easily influence us without our knowledge by suggesting ideas in our mind, awakening vital desires, and enhancing physical habits.

The fourth category requires more detailed explanations. According to many sources, at least one reptilian race existed on Earth before human beings. These first ones started to interact with humanity. Some male reptilians mated with human females and created hybrid descendents. As with donkeys and horses, which are two different species, it is possible to have a hybrid human being/intelligent non-human being lineage. The offsprings are often sterile or reproduce with difficulty. This race of ***hybrid human beings*** still exists today. The purest specimens are all members of the blue blood families that presently rule the world, such as royalty and important members of governmental, financial, banking, corporative, media, artistic, musical, sportive, and scientific spheres. 100 percent of the elite presently organizing the New World Order is made up of hybrid human beings. Their genetic code allows them to be telepathically controlled by reptilian intelligent non-human beings. Researchers such as David Icke have clearly demonstrated that people such as Elizabeth II, Bush father and son, Obama and the like are literally possessed by reptilian beings. Some types of intelligent non-human beings are then able to control what happens on Earth by subtly influencing the top members of the human herd hierarchy.

ET, IT and some extrasensorials live for a very long time, and their civilisations have existed for millions of years. Most intelligent non-human beings reproduce naturally or artificially; they have physical, technological, vital and mental powers that may seem superhuman and allow them to travel through walls, appear and disappear at will, communicate by telepathy, paralyze human beings, displace objects, and so on.

Realise that each type of intelligent non-human being has its own agenda, which either facilitates our own survival or hinders it. In the first case, we call them "good" or "benevolent." In the second case, they are classified as "evil" or "malevolent." Historically, the most cruel and ugly intelligent non-human beings – according to human standards – were classified by religions as being demons (devils, djinnṣ, *asura*) and often consisted of reptilian, insect-like or other non-human-looking beings. Beautiful, human-like and sometimes wise ET and IT were classified as angels and archangels (*deva*). These humanoid races were often taller than humans and some had blond hair, blue eyes, white skin and, occasionally, a luminous body.

Several groups of ET and IT have joined hands (and claws?) with the human world elite to form what Michael Salla calls the military-industrial-extraterrestrial complex. This military-industrial-extraterrestrial complex has been planning a New World Order based on a microchipped population that is meant to become the enslaved herd of a ruling elite that is entirely made up of hybrid human beings. These last ones would be telepathically controlled (possessed) by power-hungry extrasensorials. Other groups of intelligent non-human beings claim to be benevolent and offer to help humanity escape from this long-planned agenda. They visit some of us (Billy Myer) in their UFO or contact us telepathically (channelling) to offer their recommendations.

This division between good and bad intelligent non-human beings is strictly a creation in our image and likeness. This duality exists inside of us, human beings, and we project it onto other beings. No intelligent non-human being or human being is ever good or bad. They and we all act according to our level of consciousness. The problem is that I still perceive myself as a victim, a powerless sheep needing a shepherd (government, good intelligent non-human beings) that will protect me from the big bad wolf (bad intelligent non-human beings). Basically, it is an identity crisis.

Who is "Homo sapiens"?

The amount of disinformation about ET, IT, and extrasensorials is mind-boggling, but the one that exists concerning the true nature of human beings has even more severe repercussions. Indeed, who are we? Minerals, plants, animals, human beings, ET, IT, extrasensorials and hybrid human beings are all made up of one single creative vibration that we choose here to call Idessa.[3] This universal conscience represents all that is unmanifested (spirit) and manifested (matter). Three increasingly denser vibratory realms are used to express matter: mental, vital (emotional, astral) and physical. The thousands of types of intelligent beings that exist are made up of various combinations of these material vibrations.

Each living species in the cosmos owns a ***collective soul***, whose role is to govern it and ensure its survival. Rocks, plants, animals, ET and IT all have collective souls, along with the extrasensorials who have supraphysical bodies (physical vibrations that most humans are unable to perceive). Human beings are different for one important reason: their body is a GMO made up of an extreme genetic mixture. When ET created them out of a mixture of 22 different species, human beings found themselves connected to 22 different collective souls, each with its own agenda. Some of these souls had extremely low, "demonic" vibrations, while others had very high "angelic" frequencies. Human beings were gradually forced to shut off these conflicting voices and to live without any collective species soul. Instead, human beings started listening to the embryonic ***individual soul*** that was present in their body. That is how a new level of consciousness began to evolve.

From life to life, this soul spark grew and became what Aurobindo and The Mother (Mirra Alfassa) call a "psychic being." According to them, planet Earth is the only place in the universe where the "individual soul" experience is taking place, and humanity is presently the only species that is able to fulfil the goal of this long-planned agenda.

The development of this individual soul usually takes thousands of years and hundreds of human lives. In the meantime, a human being cannot be left on her own, without a guide connected to the world of Spirit, the highest idessic vibration. As the messages from her individual soul are still very difficult to hear, the human mind develops an ***ego*** that serves as a temporary regent for a single life. Each new incarnation ends when the body dies of fear and exhaustion. The physical body dissolves, followed by the vital body (emotional, astral), then the mental body (often mistakenly called the "spiritual" body). The ego usually dissolves with them. All that is left is the individual soul, which creates another body for yet another life, so it can continue its evolution in matter until it becomes a full-fledged "psychic being."

Homo sapiens as we know it is on the verge of becoming extinct. Humanity is simply a transition between animality and idessity, between the government of the mind and the governance of the soul. Inside each human being, a brand new idessic being is being formed. Basically, we are pregnant with our next body, as the fish was pregnant with the salamander. The behaviour of this new idessic being will not be based on intelligence – the mind – but on unlimited idessic attributes – the soul. This transition is almost over. ***No human being will survive this transformation.***

Personocratia's Path

From the ashes of the old *Homo sapiens* will actually emerge two different species. The first one will be made up of who refuse to change and to let go of the outmoded human behaviour. These human beings will simply die and reincarnate into a more harmonious species much like that of dolphins or whales. Some have already named it *Homo luminous*. This species will eventually give rise to what many prophets describe as the Golden Age. It will be the end of duality, fear and war. Will it be on Earth or elsewhere? It is hard to know.

The second species, even more mysterious, corresponds to the aim of the whole *Homo sapiens* experiment and, possibly, the ultimate purpose of the entire evolution of consciousness in matter up to now. It represents Aurobindo's "supramental being" and Teilhard de Chardin's "Omega Man." Ghis calls it the "idessic being" and symbolises it as a winged mare, as it can run on the land (matter) and fly in the air (spirit). This new being will appear on Earth very soon. It will no longer be an intelligent animal. No scientific species name will be given to it. In this ***idessic being***, the physical body, the soul and the spirit will have fused into a triunal being (three in one). The body will be made of a new matter, denser than diamond and lighter than gas, thus uniting the duality matter-spirit and creating a new, third position: the idessic being. No longer gendered, "*It*" will express all the attributes of the Supreme Being, Idessa, on an individual basis: omnipotence, immortality, omniscience, pure love, joy and peace.

The whole purpose of the *Homo sapiens* experiment is the birth of this idessic being. No *Homo luminous* and no Golden Age can exist before its manifestation. The hell-on-earth we are presently experimenting will not cease until this aim has been reached.

How can it be achieved? A critical mass of human beings needs to consciously make a transfer of power from the government of ego to the governance of soul. This means giving priority to the feminine principle (spirit) over the masculine (matter). That's the key! That allows them to clearly hear the messages from their individual souls and use their ***free will*** to obey its instructions.

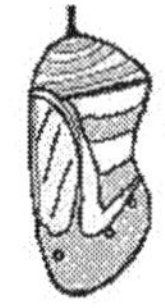

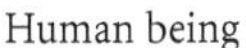

Human being Personocratia Idessic being

Ghis calls such conscious human beings ***personocratias***. They remember who they are, Idessa, and behave as such in their daily life. They are aware that their souls are connected at all times with the world of truth and know exactly the action they need to take at each moment. They know that their body is transforming into a totally new being who will no longer need to breathe, eat, reproduce or rely on any other basic animal requirements. *Personocratias* work purposefully and diligently to dissolve their egos and give complete free rein to their souls. The instructions vary from one soul to the next, as this is an individual process. When a critical mass of *personocratias* is reached, the whole universe will be affected. Idessic life will become a novel state in matter, a new expression of Idessa that will be both individual and collective: the One and the All.

Comparing Human Beings and Other Intelligent Beings

Now that we know the purpose of humanity, we can look at the New World Order, the state of our planet, the unrelenting violence and cruelty of human beings and some ET and IT in a new light. Let us examine some old belief systems.

SUPPOSITION #1: *Human beings are the only humanoids in the universe. The other intelligent species (ET, IT, extrasensorials) are very different in appearance.*

TRUTH: Several species of ET and IT are human-looking. Here are some places where they are found: *Sirius A* and *B, Nibiru, Vega, Lyra, Pleiades, Rigel, Procyon, Tau Ceti, Andromeda, Umma, Alpha Centauri*. Some look so much like human beings that we can hardly tell the difference. Others are giants or have blue, white, red, green or yellow skin. Some temporarily or permanently inhabit hidden bases on Earth and use their similar appearance to mix with local human populations. That might explain historical accounts of beings such as Krishna, Saint-Germain, Jesus or other superhuman "masters." However, human beings are the only ones to own an individual soul. This explains their very different behaviour.

SUPPOSITION #2: *Human beings are not as intelligent and wise as intelligent non-human beings, because they are a new, less-evolved species in dire need of guidance. They cannot function by themselves.*

TRUTH: Human beings are the only ones with an individual soul. They have a direct and personal contact with Idessa, the unique creative vibration. This allows them to be more conscious – they can more easily tell true from false. They are said to have ***free will.*** They can choose to listen to their individual soul bathing in the supramental world of truth, outside of all space-time limits, or to follow the ego's collective program in the world of illusion, with its restrictive natural, religious, and political laws. All intelligent non-human beings are guided by collective souls. They are more limited than human beings because their soul can only express itself in a collective manner. At the individual level, they can only function through limitative mental, vital and physical expressions that are typical of the world of fear and death.

SUPPOSITION #3: *Human beings are less evolved technologically. Advanced knowledge offered by ET is absolutely necessary to save our planet and our species.*

TRUTH: We are not facing a technological or environmental crisis, but an evolutive one. The future of humanity does not depend on more advanced technologies. We need to abandon the old *Homo sapiens* to liberate the new idessic species imprisoned inside of us.

SUPPOSITION #4: *Intelligent non-human beings are more evolved spiritually. They live in peace and love and can guide human beings so that Earth becomes a paradise.*

TRUTH: Intelligent non-human beings enjoy the false peace and codependant love typical of a herd-like hierarchy. The law of the fittest has become the law of the most intelligent and technologically advanced. It is easy for intelligent non-human beings to be generous and pacific when they can quickly dominate any rebellious member of the herd. Depending on the species, the most powerful impose their will using physical force (muscles, weapons), vital power (black magic) or mental strength (white magic). Each time, the weakest cannot do what he would like. Disorder ensues and death becomes inevitable. When a human being chooses the personocratic path, he works by contagion. By listening to her soul at all times, its psychic vibrations spread throughout her whole body. This frequency of true power, knowledge, peace, joy and love imposes a new order in her body and all of surrounding matter.

SUPPOSITION #5: *The other intelligent species in the cosmos all had to go through the same evolution stages as humanity before finally being granted access to the Cosmic Community. When human beings become more intelligent and wise, we will finally be able to join them.*

TRUTH: The purpose of humanity was never to join a Cosmic Community made up of the union of various types of intelligent and wise intelligent non-human beings. On the contrary, it is our duty to leave the old government of the mind for the new governance of the soul. Humanity is simply a transitory species between the first and the last.

SUPPOSITION #6: *Since the creation of humanity, genetic experimentation to create new human beings or modify existing human DNA has stopped.*

TRUTH: Certain IT, often guided by extrasensorials, have continued their genetic experiments on Earth. Some experimentation is done in cooperation with human scientists. The hybrid human elite also have projects of their own. In several US Army bases, witnesses have reported seeing humans (men, women, and children) in cages and a whole array of partially human "beasts." Promising embryos are raised in artificial wombs or implanted in women who are either kept in cages in situ or abducted and later released, with their memories modified. The hybrids produced in such ways are used as an elite private force of supersoldiers or to fill various positions of power within society. Cloning important leaders allows the hybrid human being ruling elite to replace non-cooperative leaders by an identical double totally under the control of the military-industrial-extraterrestrial complex. Basically, our leaders are not entirely human. We cannot expect them to understand what is going on with human evolution. Hybrid human beings can only act according to their limited view of reality, which is greatly influenced by the hive mentality characteristic of their genetic make-up.

Why Do They Come on Earth?

Intelligent non-human beings have been watching us, and many have been interacting with us for millenia. Some alien scientists have been studying members of the same human and hybrid human being families from one generation to the next, through the use of implants and abductions. The extraterrestrial geneticists who created us probably did not realize the capital role the human species would eventually play in the idessic evolution. Their collective soul was guiding them and knew the transitional role of human beings, but not the individual ET getting the work done.

With time, intelligent non-human beings noticed that the evolution of human beings was as fast as it was dramatic. They had never seen a species more violent, cruel, loving, artistic, musical, poetic… This strange new species called *Homo sapiens* was expressing the most extreme behaviour between its members and toward the rest of creation. Its individualistic tendencies were totally opposed to the survival of the species and the hive mentality typical of all animals, intelligent or otherwise. Worse still, this individualism seemed to increase exponentially with time!

Many types of intelligent non-human beings flocked to observe us. Some decided to try and help us (service-to-others types), and others, to use us for their own purposes (service-to-self types). Today, we still remain an enigmatic species for most of them.

Each intelligent non-human being species visits the Earth for different reasons. Some reptilian intraterrestrials lived on Earth long before we were created. They have been observing us and manipulating us subtly for thousands of years, making sure that the Earth will stay viable for them. Another, more advanced species of giant humanoids, the Annunaki, were the ones who came to perform genetic experiments and introduce human beings on Earth, much to the dismay of Earth's other intelligent inhabitants.

Certain intelligent non-human beings come on Earth to feed on human being physically (muscles, organs, blood, often from children) or emotionally (vital energy, also called *prana* or *chi*). Others want to take some of the natural resources found on Earth (water, minerals, DNA from plants, animals or human beings). Cosmic psychologists wish to study us, and cosmic teachers – to enlighten us in the direction they deem best for us. Some intelligent non-human beings understand that we are on the verge of a quantum leap in consciousness. They have looked into the future and found that at some point all goes blank (around 2012?). Time stops! And the problem seems to come from Earth! Consequently, some are attempting *(1)* to stop our evolution; others *(2)* to observe what will happen; and still others *(3)* to assist us as best as they can.

No intelligent non-human being can stop the human purpose from being fulfilled some day. Most do not realize that they can no longer help us and that those who attempt to stop us can only accelerate the process. *Nothing can stop Idessa!* The Apocalypse, the "uncovering" is well under way. We have almost reached the crucial point where the adventure becomes totally individual and each one of us must perform her internal transformation alone. Those who refuse to change and to let go of the outmoded human behaviour will simply die and reincarnate into the *Homo luminous* mentioned earlier.

How Should I Behave with Them?

Now that I finally understand the human agenda, it is time to stop putting intelligent non-human beings on a pedestal, should it be spiritual or scientific. Each intelligent species in the cosmos fulfils its own purpose in the universal idessic dance, guided by her collective soul. Each human being has her own purpose, which is totally different and steered by her individual soul.

However, some pieces of the puzzle still need to be addressed. Since at least 1930, and possibly before, certain ET have offered precise technological information to a small elite of human beings. The military-industrial complex, first mentioned by Eisenhower, truly exists, but he deliberately forgot to mention the third player: ET. This past US president surely knew of their existence since he had met on several instances with at least two ET species and made deals with one of them in 1954. Before him, other leaders, such as Hitler, have done the same.

Because of reverse engineering of crashed UFO and alien vehicles offered by ET, the hybrid human being elite ruling over the military-industrial-extraterrestrial complex now owns its own fleets of UFO. These will be used to help the secret elite establish the New World Order more efficiently. The military-industrial-extraterrestrial complex is also responsible for a good part of human being abductions. They kidnap those who were previously abducted by ET because they are trying to understand the reason for the ET's intensive multigenerational studies. On their side, ET are desperately attempting to understand and harness the incredible power of individual souls. Basically, they want to have access to human beings' potential for unlimited powers without going through the human incarnation process, as this would mean loosing all mental and technological powers, and their long lifespan. ET are trying to avoid the need to go back to square one and to suffer through a continuous series of human lives that can only be experienced as hell-on-earth.

In the coming years, the military-industrial-extraterrestrial complex has planned a false worldwide extraterrestrial invasion, using its secret fleets of UFO. This event will probably be preceded by *(1)* a global economic crisis, *(2)* a global pandemic, and *(3)* a third world war. They may also simulate the arrival of a holographic Christ-like saviour, using another type of secret technology. This scenario is called the ***Blue Beam Project***. The combination of all these events will trigger the establishment of a New World Order, combining both the spiritual (religion) and temporal (politics) aspects into the hands of a single world dictator. When we think about the incredible amount of disinformation surrounding the exopolitical phenomenon, it becomes obvious that the hybrid elite now running the world in secret will use this master card at the very end of its conspirational poker game.

Conclusion

When we study the innumerable reports from human beings who have been in contact with intelligent non-human beings, it becomes obvious that the intelligent beings who visit us and possess physical bodies are all mortal, even if most live for a very long time. They also eat physical, vital or mental food. Most need to reproduce, wear clothes and use technological tools to travel around and accomplish various tasks. All believe in an external god and universal/cosmic laws. Some of them respect these laws and others choose to break them. Even if they travel in time (past and future), they remain captive of the illusory world of space-time, which is based on fear and death. Thus, we can conclude that intelligent non-human beings belong to two large categories of beings. They are either ***superbly intelligent animals*** governed by a collective soul, or ***disincarnate beings*** without a physical body (some extrasensorials). A third possibility would be to have a ***combination*** of both: animal-bodied ET and IT who are possessed and ruled by extrasensorials. Remember that our hybrid human being ruling elite are also controlled by extrasensorials. Most human beings are also affected by the subtle power of extrasensorials. Their influence can be stopped, but we must first be aware of the problem.

Human beings are also intelligent animals, but each one is governed by an individual soul, allowing to create the passage between animality and idessity. From the very cells of human beings will emerge idessic beings: Idessa individualized. In such idessic bodies, everything becomes possible and all laws fall apart. This unique event is now under intense preparation inside all human beings who accept to place their bodies totally under the governance of their soul. Each of these courageous human beings follow a pathless path, where nothing from the past or from other planets, star systems, galaxies or any parallel universe can guide them.

It is now clear that intelligent non-human beings represent our evolutive past. Thousands of years ago, the bravest ones among them chose to start the long process of consecutive incarnations inside human bodies. A lot of courage was needed, since incarnating as a *Homo sapiens* means accepting to be born totally unconscious and to live a life of intense suffering. The ceaseless physical torture, emotional distress and mental torment represent the diving boards allowing us to leap into the unknown world of the new species. Worse still, each human being needs to discover an individual path to idessic life in matter.

Evolution always happens inside bodies. In the past, these bodies were unconscious of the reason for the change from one form to another. Fish did not choose wilfully to become salamanders. Most probably, there was a simple switch from the voice of one collective soul to the next. For human beings, it is an entirely new procedure, based on conscious free will. Those who dare work hard to dissolve the old survival ego. ***No intelligent non-human being can help them in any way*** – only their soul knows the way to succeed.

If I choose the personocratic path, I must *(1)* call and listen to my own individual soul, *(2)* give her free rein to run my life, and *(3)* surrender to her requests. The greatest difficulty is to perceive the difference between my ego's voice, which insists on following the animal program and on insuring the survival of the species, and that of my soul, which follows its individual path and aspires to fulfil its long-awaited plan.

The issue is collective, but the answer, individual. One thing is sure: ***nothing can stop Idessa.*** It is truly the end of *Homo sapiens* and the beginning of a new ways of being. I can decide to participate in the process or to hang on to an outmoded program. Do or die!

Published in issue 4 of The Dot Connector magazine (July-August 2009).

Project Blue Beam

Serge Monast (1945-1996)

> Serge Monast and another journalist, both of whom were researching Project Blue Beam died of "heart attacks" within weeks of each other, although neither had a history of heart disease. Serge was in Canada. The other Canadian journalist was visiting Ireland. Prior to his death, the "unknown" commandos abducted Serge's daughter in an attempt to dissuade him from pursuing his research into Project Blue Beam. His daughter was never returned...
>
> — *Ken Adachi, Educate-Yourself.org*

The infamous NASA (National Aeronautics and Space Administration) *Blue Beam Project* has *four different steps* in order to implement the New Age religion with the Antichrist at its head. *We must remember that the New Age religion is the very foundation for the new world government*, without which religion the dictatorship of the New World Order is completely impossible. I'll repeat: *Without a universal belief in the New Age religion, the success of the New World Order will be impossible!* That is why the Blue Beam Project is so important to them, but has been so well hidden until now.

Engineered Earthquakes and Hoaxed "Discoveries"

The first step in the NASA Blue Beam Project concerns the breakdown (reevaluation) of all archaeological knowledge. It deals with the set-up, with artificially created earthquakes at certain precise locations on the planet, of *supposedly new discoveries* which will finally explain to all people the "error" of all fundamental religious doctrines. The falsification of this information will be used to make all nations believe that their religious doctrines have been misunderstood for centuries and misinterpreted. Psychological preparations for that first step have already been implemented with the film, *2001: A Space Odyssey*, the *StarTrek* series, and *Independence Day*, all of which deal with invasions from space and the coming together of all nations to repel the invaders. The later films, such as *Jurrassic Park*, deal with the theories of evolution and claim God's words are lies.[1]

What is important to understand in the first step is that those earthquakes will hit at different parts of the world where scientific and archaeological teachings have indicated that arcane mysteries have been buried. By those types of earthquakes, it will be possible for scientists to rediscover those mysteries which will be used to discredit all fundamental religious doctrines. This is the first preparation for the plan for humanity, because *what they want to do is destroy the beliefs of all Christians and Muslims on the planet.* To do that, they need some *false "proof" from the far past* that will prove to all nations that their religions have all been misinterpreted and misunderstood.

The Big Space Show in the Sky

The second step in the NASA Blue Beam Project involves a gigantic 'space show' with three-dimensional optical holograms and sounds, laser projection of multiple *holographic images* to different parts of the world, each receiving a different image according to predominating regional national religious faith. This new "god's" voice will be speaking in all languages.

In order to understand that, we must study various secret services' research done in the last 25 years.

The Soviets have perfected the advanced computer systems, even exported them, and fed them with the minute physio-psychological particulars based on their studies of the anatomy and electromechanical composition of the human body, and the studies of the electrical, chemical and biological properties of the human brain. These computers were fed, as well, with the languages of all human cultures and their meanings. The dialects of all cultures have been fed into the computers from satellite transmissions.

The Soviets began to feed the computers with objective programs like the ones of the new messiah. It also seems that the Soviets – the New World Order people – have resorted to suicidal methods with the human society by allocating electronic wavelengths for every person and every society and culture to induce suicidal thoughts if the person doesn't comply with the dictates of the New World Order.

There are two different aspects of step two. The first is the *"space show."* Where does the space show come from? The space show, the holographic images will be used in a simulation of the ending during which all nations will be shown scenes that will be the fulfillment of that which they desire to verify the prophecies and adversary events.

These will be projected from satellites onto the sodium layer about 60 miles above the earth. We see tests every once in a while, but they are called "UFOs" and "flying saucers" sightings.

The result of these deliberately staged events will be to show the world the new "Christ," the new messiah, *Matraia* (Maitreya), for the immediate implementation of the new world religion. *Enough truth will be foisted upon an unsuspecting world to hook them into the lie.* "Even the most learned will be deceived."

The project has perfected the ability for some device to *lift up an enormous number of people*, as in a *rapture*, and whisk the entire group into a never-never land. We see tests of this device in the abduction of humans by those mysterious little alien greys who snatch people out of their beds and through windows into waiting "mother ships." The calculated resistance to the universal religion and the new messiah and the ensuing holy wars will result in the loss of human life on a scale never imagined before in all of human history.

The Blue Beam Project will pretend to be the *universal fulfillment of the prophecies of old*, as major an event as that which occurred 2,000 years ago. In principle, it will make use of the *skies as a movie screen* (on the sodium layer at about 60 miles) as *space-based laser-generating satellites project simultaneous images to the four corners of the planet in every language and dialect according to the region.* It deals with the religious aspect of the New World Order and is deception and seduction on a massive scale.

Computers will coordinate the satellites, and software already in place will run the sky show. Holographic images are based on nearly identical signals combining to produce an image or hologram with deep perspective which is equally applicable to acoustic ELF, VLF and LF waves and optical phenomena. Specifically, the show will consist of multiple holographic images to different parts of the world, each receiving a different image according to the specific national, regional religion.

Not a single area will be excluded. With computer animation and sounds appearing to emanate from the very depths of space, astonished ardent followers of the various creeds will witness their own returned messiahs *in convincing lifelike reality.*

Then the projections of Jesus, Mohammed, Buddha, Krishna, etc., will merge into one after correct explanations of the mysteries and revelations will have been disclosed. This one god will, in fact, be the Antichrist, who will explain that the various scriptures have been misunderstood and misinterpreted, and that the religions of old are responsible for turning brother against brother, and nation against nation, therefore old religions must be abolished to make way for the New Age new world religion, representing the one god Antichrist they see before them.

Naturally, this superbly staged falsification will result in dissolved social and religious disorder on a grand scale, each nation blaming the other for the deception, *setting loose millions of programmed religious fanatics* through demonic possession on a scale never witnessed before. In addition, *this event will occur at a time of profound worldwide political anarchy and general tumult created by some worldwide catastrophe.*

The United Nations even now plan to use Beethoven's "Song of Joy" as the anthem for the introduction for the New Age one world religion.

If we put this space show in parallel with the star wars program, we get this: combination of electromagnetic radiation and hypnosis which have also been the subject of intensive research. In 1974, for instance, researcher G. F. Shapits, said of one of the research proposals that, "... *in this investigation it will be shown that the spoken words of the hypnotist may also be converted by electromagnetic energy directly and to the subconscious part of the human brain without employing any mechanical device for receiving or transcording the message, and without the person exposed to such influence having a chance to control the information input consciously. ... The rationalized behavior will be considered to have been taken out of their own free will.*"

Anyone investigating so-called "channelling" phenomena right now would be wise to take this area of research into consideration. It will be noted that those who think of themselves as 'channellers' have escalated rapidly since this type of research was conducted. It is uncanny how similar their messages are, despite which entity they claim to be their source of divine guidance. It would suggest any individual considering the credibility of channelled information should be discerning and critically evaluate where the message they are receiving originates, and if the messages are specifically beneficial to the New World Order.

The *Sydney Morning* newspaper published an item on March 21st, 1983, which announced that the Soviets were invading the human mind, the article having been submitted to the foreign editor by *Doctor Nathan Abnuengy*, assistant professor in the faculty of agriculture in Asia. It is worth quoting the article at length even though his grammar is a little old. This article relates to the Soviets who created the supercomputer we were discussing earlier and which is really important because these types of computers can be run through satellites and through space. The computers were fed with all the different languages and their meanings, the dialect of all peoples were fed to the computers with objective programs. But we are no longer talking about the Soviets; we are talking about the *United Nations*, the minions of the New World Order, who are feeding the computers with the necessary information.

The editor of the column in which the article appeared even states that the piece made points too important to ignore. I think it is possible that the persons who have created this mega-mind-control-program could sell the software to an organization and not be aware that the client might use the program and data to enslave all of humankind. Just imagine how far they have advanced since that article was published!

Artificial Thought and Communication

The advancement of techniques propels us toward the third step in the Blue Beam Project that goes along with the telepathic and electronically augmented two-way communication where ELF, VLF and LF waves will reach each person from within his or her own mind, convincing each of them that their own god is speaking to them from the very depths of their own soul. Such rays from satellites are fed from the memories of computers that have stored massive data about every human on earth, and their languages. The rays will then interlace with their natural thinking to form what we call diffuse artificial thought.

That kind of technology goes into the 1970s, 1980s, and 1990s research where the human brain has been compared to a computer. Information is fed in, processed, integrated and then a response is formulated and acted upon. Mind controllers manipulate information the same way a computer for grammar manipulates information. In January 1991, the University of Arizona hosted a conference entitled, "*The NATO Advanced*

Research Workshop on Current and Emergent Phenomena and Biomolecular Systems." What does that mean exactly? It means this: We refer to one paper that was delivered at the conference which stands out for its different attitude towards the development under discussion at that time. It was, in effect, a protest and chilling warning to the attending scientists about the potential abuse of their research findings.

Their findings, of course, stated that the United States has already developed communications equipment which can make the blind see, the deaf hear and the lame walk. It can relieve the terminally ill from pain without the use of drugs or surgery. I'm not talking about science fiction. A man might retain the use of all his faculties right up to the moment of his death.

This communications equipment depends upon a completely new way of looking at the human brain and neuromuscular systems and radiation pulses at ultra-low frequencies. Some of this equipment is now operational within the CIA and FBI. It will never be used to make the blind see, the deaf hear and the lame walk because it is central to the domestic political agenda and foreign policy of George Bush and his puppet-masters of the New World Order.

Domestically, the new communications equipment is being used to torture and murder persons who match profiles imagined to be able to screen a given population for terrorists; to torture and murder citizens who belong to organizations which promote tolerance and peace and development in Central America; to torture and murder citizens who belong to organizations who oppose the development and deployment of nuclear weapons, and to create a race of slave cult automatons, or what is popularly called "the Manchurian Candidates."

Overseas experimentation is taking place on hostages held by the United States and Canada, Great Britain, Australia, Germany, Finland and France. Additionally, *there has been a long series of bizarre suicides among British computer scientists, all of whom have had some connection to the United States Navy.*

What is possible to ask before such a psychology of terror is this: would any government, corporation or psychiatrist wilfully promote such horror today? The answer is quite obviously, "Yes."

Government agencies and the corporations that work with them toward New World Order are prepared to promote anything that will help them achieve their objective of total social control.

As for the question of why. For one thing, if you terrify the public and make them fear for their safety, they will allow you to implement draconian law enforcement practice, disarm them and keep extensive records on them, and they only have to tell you that it is all to protect you, of course. Secondly, it promotes the decay of the present democratic forms of political systems and leads societies to search for alternative methods of political ideology. Of course, *the alternative has already been planned.* It is called the New World Order and it will not have your safety or interests at heart. As George Bush said: "Read my lips." Fear has always been used by powerful elite to control and subjugate the masses.

The old maxim, "divide and conquer," is being played out to the limit worldwide to ensure that everyone is frightened for their personal safety, and to be suspicious of everyone else. This, too, is mind control.

To go further in regard to the new technology which is at the base of the Blue Beam Project, we have to consider this statement by psychologist James V. McConnell which was published in a 1970s issue of *Psychology Today.* He said, *"The day has come when we can combine sensory deprivation with drug hypnosis and astute manipulation of reward and punishment to gain almost absolute control over an individual's behavior. It should then be possible to achieve a rapid and highly effective type of positive brainwashing that would allow us to make dramatic changes in a person's behavior and personality."*

Now, when we talked before about that kind of ray and the telepathic and electronically augmented communication, the kind of rays that are fed from the memories of computers which store massive data about humans, human language and dialects, and we said that the people will be reached from within, making each person to believe that his god is speaking from within his or her own soul, we refer to that kind of technology and that kind of thinking that same psychologist was espousing, that is: we should be trained from birth that we should do what society wants us to do rather than what we ourselves want to do; that because they have the technology to do it, *no one should now be allowed to have their own individual personality.*

This statement and these ideas are important because it is the basic teaching of the United Nations that no one owns his or her own personality. And that same psychologist claims that no one has any say-so about the kind of personality they acquire and there is no reason to believe you have the right to refuse to acquire a new personality if your old personality is considered "antisocial."

What is important in this declaration is that the New World Order will be set up over the current system, meaning the old way of thinking and behavior and religion will be considered the "old" and incorrect way of thinking and that they can change it at one of the *eradication camps*[2] of the United Nations to make sure that anyone with this "antisocial" behavior will be disposed of quickly so that other modified individuals will be able to fulfill the needs and agendas of the New World Order without being distracted by the truth.

Could this be the greatest mind control project ever?

The NASA Blue Beam Project is the prime directive for the New World Order's absolute control over the populations of the entire Earth. I would suggest you investigate this information carefully before dismissing it as fanatic lunacy. If we go further in the different reports we have presented, we find that the mind control operations and technology include a transmitter that broadcasts *at the same frequency as the human nervous system*, which transmitter is manufactured by the *Loral Electro-Optical Systems* in Pasadena, California.

Loral, a major defense contractor, has previously conducted research on directed energy weapons for Lt. Gen. Leonard Perez of the US Air Force who was searching for a weapon that could implant messages into the minds of the enemy while urging his own troops on to superhuman deeds of valor! The device employs electromagnetic radiation of gigahertz frequencies (microwaves) pulsed at extremely low frequencies (ELF). It is used to torture people both physically and mentally from a distance.

Weapons of this type are thought to have been used against a British woman protesting the presence of American cruise missiles at Greenham Common Airbase during the 1970s. This weapon can be used to induce total sensory deprivation by broadcasting signals into the auditory nerve at such high power that it blocks the ability of the individual to hear themselves think!

The process employed by such ELF technology are described in various US Defense Department publications, including one entitled, "*The Electromagnetic Spectrum and Low Intensity Conflict*," by Captain Paul E. Tyler, Medical Commandant, US Navy, which is included in a collection entitled, "*Low Intensity Conflict and Modern Technology Edict*," by Lt. Col David G. Dean, USAF. The paper was delivered in 1984, and the collection published in 1986 by Air University Press, Maxwell Airforce Base, Alabama.

Another pulse microwave device can deliver audible signals directly to an individual while remaining undetectable to anyone else. The technology is very simple and can be built by using an ordinary police radar gun. The microwave beam generated by the device is modulated at audio frequencies and can broadcast messages directly into the brain. Now here we come to the NASA Blue Beam Project. The broadcasting of subliminal two-way communication and images from the depths of space correspond directly to that kind of technology.

In his book, *The Body Electric,* Nobel Prize nominee Dr. Robert O. Becker describes a series of experiments conducted in the early 1960s by Allen Frie, where this phenomena was demonstrated, as well as later experiments conducted in 1973 at the Walter Reed Army Institute of Research by Dr. Joseph C. Sharp who personally underwent tests in which he proved he could hear and understand messages delivered to him in an echo-free isolation chamber via a pulsed microwave audiogram, which is an analog of the word's sound vibration beamed into his brain. Becker then goes on to state, "*Such a device has obvious application for covert operations designed to drive a target crazy with unknown voices or deliver undetectable instructions to a programmed assassin.*"

Now figure out when we hear that voice from the New World messiah who would be speaking from space to all of the sane (?) people of the earth who might give instructions to zealots and religious fanatics, we would see hysteria and social mayhem on a scale never witnessed before on this planet. *No police forces in the world, even as a combined front, could deal with the disorder that will follow!*

A 1978 book entitled *Microwave Auditory Effect and Application,* by James C. Lynn, describes how *audible voices can be broadcast directly into the brain.* This technology could actually allow the blind to see and the deaf to hear. Instead, it has been turned into a weapon to enslave the world.

Allen Frie also reports that he could speed up, slow down or stop the hearts of isolated frogs by synchronizing the pulsed rate of a microwave beam with the heart itself. According to Dr. Robert Becker, similar results have been obtained using live frogs, which shows that *it is technically feasible to produce* ***heart attacks*** *with rays designed to penetrate the human chest.*

[EDITOR'S NOTE: *Both the author of this report and his colleague died of "heart attacks" only days apart. We should mention also that Dr. Becker does not participate in such research.*]

It has been demonstrated that focused ultra high frequency (UHF) electromagnetic energy beams can be used to induce considerable agitation and muscular activity or induce muscular weakness and lethargy. Microwaves can also be used to burn human skin and aid the effect of drugs, bacteria and poisons or affect the function of the entire brain. These effects were all revealed at length by the CIA on September 21, 1977 in testimony before the Subcommittee on Health and Scientific Research. Dr. Sidney Gottlieb who directed the *MKULTRA* program at that time, was forced to discuss the scope of the CIA's research to find techniques of activation of the human organism by remote electronic means. So this is something that exists right now, that has been pursued to its highest degree, that can be used from space to reach any person, anyplace on the face of the Earth.

If we go deeper in that process of mind control over the people we find that the equipment and technology has been used to influence politics in a much more direct fashion. Michael Dukakis, the Democrat candidate running against George Bush in the 1988 election was targeted with microwave technology in order to impede his public speaking performance once the public opinion polls showed he posed a serious threat to Bush's election prospects. He also claims that the equipment was used against Kitty Dukakis and drove her to the brink of suicide. In the Disneyland world of US politics, a presidential candidate with problems such as these, would obviously lose their race to the White House.

In the December 1980 edition of the US Army journal, called the *Military Review*, a column by Lt. Col. John B. Alexander, entitled "*The New Mental Battlefield: Beam Me Up, Spock,*" provides further insight into the technical capabilities at the disposal of the controller. He writes:

"Several examples will demonstrate areas in which progress have been made. The transference of energy from one organism to another; the ability to heal ***or cause disease to be transmitted over a distance, thus inducing illness or death from no apparent cause;*** *telepathic behavior modification which includes the ability to induce hypnotic states up to a distance of 1,000 kilometers have been reported.*

The use of telepathic hypnosis also holds great potential. This capability could allow agents to be deeply planted with no conscious knowledge of their programming."

In movie terms, the Manchurian Candidate lives, and does not even require a telephone call.

"Other mind-to-mind induction techniques are being considered. If perfected, this capability could allow the direct transference of thought via telepathy from one mind or group of minds to a select target audience. The unique factor is that the recipient will not be aware that thought has been implanted from an external source. He or she will believe the thoughts are original."

This is exactly what we were talking about.

The third step in the NASA Blue Beam Project is called the *Telepathic Electronic Two-Way Communication*. Lt. Col. Alexander's article continues:

"If it is possible to feed artificial thought into the multigenic field via satellite, ***the mind control of the entire planet is now possible.*** *An individual's only resistance would be to constantly question the motivation behind their thoughts and not act upon thoughts which they consider to be outside their own ideological, religious and moral boundaries."*

Once again, it is wise to consider how television, advertising, modern education and various types of social pressure are used to manipulate those boundaries. It has been reported by Lt. Col. Alexander who said, in the summary of his *Military Review* article: *"The information on those kinds of technologies presented here would be considered by some to be ridiculous since it does not conform to their view of reality."*

But some people still believe the world is flat.

Now, this means a lot, because if people do not believe this kind of technology is possible, or think it is science fiction, those people put themselves in great jeopardy, because on the night when those thousand stars will shine from space, during the night when the New Messiah will be presented to the world, they will not be prepared and will have no time to prepare to save themselves against that kind of technology. They don't believe and they won't take time to prepare.

This is exactly what happens to people who are convinced by Satan into believing that he doesn't exist, so they have no defence against him.

Universal Supernatural Manifestations via Electronics

The fourth step concerns the universal supernatural manifestation with electronic means. It contains three different orientations.

One is to make mankind believe that an alien (off-world) invasion is about to occur at every major city on earth in order to provoke each major nation to use its nuclear weapons in order to strike back. This way, the

United Nations Court will require that all those nations which launched nuclear weapons to disarm when the invasion is shown to have been false. And how will the United Nations know that the invasion was false? They will have staged it, of course.

The second is to make the Christians believe that the rapture is going to occur with the supposed divine intervention of an alien (off-world) civilization coming to rescue earthlings from a savage and merciless demon. Its goal will be to dispose of all significant opposition to the implementation of the New World Order in one major stroke, actually within hours of the beginning of the sky show!

The third orientation in the fourth step is a mixture of electronic and supernatural forces. The waves used at that time will allow "supernatural forces" to travel through optical fibers, coaxial cables (TV), electrical and phone lines in order to penetrate to everyone at once through major appliances. Embedded chips will already be in place. The goal of this deals with global Satanic ghosts projected all around the world in order to push all populations to the edge of hysteria and madness, to drown them into a wave of suicide, murder and permanent psychological disorders. After the *Night of the Thousand Stars*, worldwide populations will be ready for the *New Messiah to re-establish order and peace at any cost*, even at the cost of abdication of freedom.

Phasing Out Cash and Independence

The techniques used in the fourth step is exactly the same used in the past in the USSR to force the people to accept Communism. The same technique will be used by the United Nations to implement the new world religion and the New World Order.

A lot of people ask when this is going to happen and how they will accomplish the visions of the Night of a Thousand Stars, and the events that will point to the days when it will begin. According to the many reports we have received, we believe *it will begin with some kind of worldwide economic disaster*. Not a complete crash, but enough to allow them to introduce some kind of in-between currency before they introduce their electronic cash to replace all paper or plastic money. The in-between currency will be used to force anyone with savings to spend or turn in their cash because they understand that people who have money and are not dependent upon them might be the very ones who will mount an insurrection against them. If everyone is broke, no one can fund a war of any kind: paper currency will cease to exist. This is one of the first signs.

But to implement the worldwide electronic money system, everyone in the world who might have money in the future, will have to have a way to transfer money electronically. Before that time, everyone will have spent all of their cash, reserves and assets. Everyone has to be 100 percent dependent upon the Council for their existence.

To prevent any kind of independence, the New World Order has already implanted microchips in wild animals, birds, fish, etc. Why? They want to make certain that the people who will not accept the New World Order will not be able to hunt or fish anywhere in the world. *If they try, they will be tracked and traced by satellites, then hunted down and imprisoned or killed.*

The New World Order is already changing the laws of all nations to make everyone dependent upon a single food and vitamin supply. They are changing laws about religion and psychiatric disorders in order to identify anyone who is potentially threatening to the NWO. Those who are found defective will be sent to *eradication camps*[2], where their *organs will be taken and sold to the highest bidders.*[3] Those who are not killed outright will be used as slave labor or used in medical experiments.

The goal of a dictatorship is to control everyone, everywhere, ruthlessly and without exception. That's why the new technology being introduced everywhere is a technology for the control of the people. The technology of the 1940s and 1950s was used to help the people have an easier and more productive life. The new technology is designed and built to track down and control people everywhere. This technology is being manufactured for a specific purpose, and to refuse to recognize that this purpose is to enslave the entire populations of the world, is to deny the emergence and the establishment of the New World Order religion and government.

If you cannot see, if you cannot learn, if you cannot understand, then you and your family and friends will succumb to the fires of the *crematoria that have been built in every state and every major city on earth,*[4] built to deal with you. No one is safe in a totalitarian police state!

Written by Serge Monast and originally published in 1994.
Published in issue 1 of The Dot Connector magazine (January-February 2009).

Awaken in the Now

Colin Bondi

"What you resist persists"... Do you find yourself resisting painful or unpleasant feelings and situations in your life? If so, what has been the result of that resistance? With acceptance we are acknowledging the reality of what is happening simply because it is what is in this moment. This doesn't mean we are giving into it in a disempowered way, but acceptance is usually a prerequisite to change. By accepting a painful situation we open the door to healing and the potential to create something different...

From Fear to Empowered Engagement

What does the current world situation bring up for you? This question produces a variety of responses depending on who you ask. There are seriously alarming things playing out right now, many of which are major global events such as climate change. Beyond that we seem to be creating increasingly oppressive governments even in our so-called free western societies. Our society, at least to me, appears to be suffering from a degenerative sickness which is entering a terminal stage. The degradation of our society is evidenced by many symptoms, including increasing extremism, a poisoning of the food supply due to genetic and toxic contamination, a healthcare system that is based on profit instead of healing and sells poison under the guise of medicine, an almost complete lack of honesty and morality in government, a numbed out population that spends its time entranced by mass media promoting extremely dysfunctional behavior and propaganda, and an economy where both greed and manufactured scarcity run rampant.

Two common responses to this, that represent two ends of a spectrum, include *indifference* or *denial*, on one end, and *anger* and *resistance*, on the other. While these two responses seem to be polar opposites, they have a common underlying basis of *fear*.

It would be quite unbelievable to honestly take a look at what is happening in the world and not experience some degree of fear. Have you allowed yourself to see and acknowledge fully what is happening? These are very challenging times, and the future has never been more uncertain, but how we see these events and how we respond are critical in determining what form this uncertainty takes.

Uncertainty, or the unknown, tends to evoke fear in human beings because of our habitual way of seeing ourselves as separate beings in a material universe. *This illusory separation is the root cause of fear.* The unknown in truth contains the limitless possibility of abundance, which is our true nature, but fear arising out of separation cuts us off from this natural abundance. This is important because if we face the current uncertainty with fear we will collectively create our worst nightmare. So what do we do if fear naturally arises in response to these trying times and it has the power to create what we least want to experience?

One possible answer to this question is to *transform our fear into empowerment*. Denying or avoiding fear only pushes it into the unconscious where it wreaks havoc on our lives causing us to feel victimized by our life situation. Acting out of fear or anger masking fear is no better because it produces results that are infused with the energy of fear and disempowerment. If, however, we recognize and acknowledge our fear, we open up the potential for transforming it. This can be done through the practice of mindfulness, which I describe in detail in ***"Mindfulness and the Practice of RAIN"*** below.

By owning our fear we not only initiate healing for ourselves, but we begin to act as healers for our society as well, because we bring empowerment instead of fear to the collective consciousness. Being aware of and accepting of our fear transforms its raw energy into conscious empowerment which we can then put to effective use to create real change.

In a state of conscious empowerment we cannot be manipulated or deceived and we directly see that we are not separate from the external world but in fact co-create it with what we think, feel and do. This co-creation of our experience can happen consciously or unconsciously, and I would say we find ourselves at a stage in our evolution where unconscious co-creation is no longer possible, it has become too destructive. With empowerment we also have a powerful impact on those around us because we touch and trigger their empowered nature even if they are not aware of it at the moment. This allows us to confront destructive behavior in a much more effective way, we don't condone it and we don't resist or fight against it, rather we confront it with fearless empowered presence. We can do this because our fear has been owned and transformed into the very power we use to create change, and we create that change by stepping into it ourselves as examples of what a fearless empowered life looks like.

We have a choice as to whether we take destructiveness to its most extreme manifestation, or whether we consciously step into our roles as divine co-creators and help shape a new, more healthy, more nurturing society. We cannot do that without facing the darker parts of ourselves, including our fear and our needs that result from past trauma. Both we as individuals and as a society are in dire need of healing, and this healing needs to start within each of us.

I think, the positive aspect of our world situation is that its pressure and intensity will not allow us to avoid this healing any longer, we cannot continue the way we have been without destroying ourselves. We can use these intense times as the fuel for change and healing if we understand how to transform our fear and let go of our separation. Then we can respond to whatever happens with empowered engagement.

Mindfulness and the Practice of RAIN

Most people have heard of mindfulness. Like meditation, it has become a fairly common term in general use. It has also become more accepted in western psychology as having therapeutic benefit. Many books have been written on the topic, and yet there remains much confusion in terms of just what mindfulness is and how to apply it on a daily basis to heal and find greater freedom. This is especially true with regard to difficult or emotional situations. It's easier to be mindful of a sunset compared to the intense anger in a fight with a partner.

While the definition of mindfulness varies, I would describe it as a *gentle, focused, compassionate attention.* A quality of spaciously noticing what is happening, whether it be within or without. In the west today there has developed a tradition of Buddhist training and practice that is mixed with western psychology. From this tradition, represented by psychologist/Buddhist teachers such as Jack Kornfield and Tara Brach, a very practical application of mindfulness practice has emerged that can be readily applied in daily life, especially with difficult issues or situations.

The acronym that describes this powerful approach is ***RAIN***. It stands for ***recognition***, ***acceptance***, ***investigation***, and ***non-identification***. The first aspect of this approach is ***recognition***, and this is where basic mindfulness comes in. If we are feeling pain or suffering, the first thing we need to do is actually be aware of it. In this fast paced society with so many distractions and ways of numbing ourselves this is often not so easy. We can carry irritation, hurt feelings and pain under the surface while we just try to get through our day, *toughing it out*. We can also carry emotional trauma from past experiences over years, which turns into depression, anxiety and illness. The practice of mindfulness begins with an intention to simply pay more attention to what is going on inside us instead of glossing over it. When we feel tense, upset, angry or discomfort of any kind we can briefly pause and check in to see what is going on. *Recognizing that we are suffering is the first step to freedom.*

The second aspect of RAIN is ***acceptance***. Recognition is not enough because we can recognize something unpleasant and then proceed to distract ourselves from it, deny it or simply wish it wasn't happening. This process takes some courage, however, and an intention to confront pain and discomfort, which usually doesn't happen until we have had the realization by experience that there is really no way to avoid what we don't want, it happens anyway, and the resistance prolongs it and makes it worse, hence the expression, "*What you resist persists.*" Do you find yourself resisting painful or unpleasant feelings and situations in your life? If so, what has been the result of that resistance? With acceptance we are acknowledging the reality of what is happening simply because it is what is in this moment. This does not mean we are giving into it in a disempowered way, but acceptance is usually a prerequisite to change. *By accepting a painful situation we open the door to healing and the potential to create something different.*

The next part of the process, after we've recognized and accepted what we're feeling, is ***investigation***, this is core of RAIN. This is the opposite of denying, avoiding or distracting. It involves looking directly into our painful feelings or experience. This is the deeper aspect of mindfulness where we stop and allow ourselves to feel and delve a bit deeper into the thoughts and feelings involved.

The Buddha described *four basic foundations* of mindfulness practice, and each of them can be employed at this stage. The first is *mindfulness of the body*. As we investigate, we can pay close attention to our body and any tension or feelings it holds. We may be experiencing tightness in the chest or an upset stomach or a headache. The body can hold pent up emotions and energy from past trauma, so it is a powerful tool to get in touch with things that need to be released as well as grounding us in the present moment. We sit and pay attention to our body and focus close gentle attention on any area that we're drawn to and feel what is there. Often, as we feel into discomfort in the body, we will experience different qualities to it, tightness in the chest may start to feel like a burning heat and then a deep sadness, a headache may begin to feel like pressure and then grief or tears. We just delve into it as deep as we can and notice and give space to whatever is there. Gentle focused attention has the effect of unfolding the initial sensation and uncovering what is beneath it allowing healing to occur.

The second foundation of mindfulness is *feeling*. The Buddha spoke of two types of feeling. Primary feelings and secondary feelings. Primary feeling comes first, and it is the quality of feeling we unconsciously project on to every single experience we have. Primary feeling is positive, negative or neutral. From this come secondary feelings, which we are more consciously aware of, including positive feelings such as physical pleasure, happiness and excitement. We also have negative feelings such as anger, jealousy, and fear, as well as neutral feelings such as numbness, laziness and confusion. These emerge from the primary feeling that was initially associated with a situation or experience, so it sets the stage for what comes next. At this stage we observe our feelings becoming aware of what we are feeling and allowing ourselves to openly feel what is there. Giving our feelings attention allows us to realize that they are just energy, and like energy they need to flow and can get blocked if we don't pay attention to them or give them space to arise.

The third foundation of mindfulness is *thought*. Here we observe the thoughts and the thought processes that are involved in the situation. We do this without indulging or judging them, we simply allow ourselves to be aware of the thoughts. This is a key aspect of mindfulness, it is a simple awareness that notices. Indulging thoughts happens when we stop noticing them and get lost in them or identify with them, and judgment is just another thought to be noticed with awareness. Mindfulness is very simple and yet very powerful, but it is so simple that we can miss seeing and experiencing how powerful it actually is. The thought aspect of this process is quite important because many of us identify with our thoughts, imagining that they represent who we are. By noticing our thoughts with awareness we free ourselves from compulsive thinking because we see that they arise, remain for a time and then dissolve while the whole time awareness remains as the watcher.

The forth foundation of mindfulness is *Dharma*. The word Dharma has a number of meanings in Buddhism, but here we can take it to mean *truth*, the deeper truth of an experience, a truth that only we can uncover within, which brings freedom. With this aspect we widen the lens of our mindfulness and look at the overall process attempting to see the truth behind it. This might include asking ourselves some questions about what we're struggling with. Am I seeing things clearly? Is there an ongoing pattern I'm playing out in this situation? Am I imagining that how I'm feeling right now will last forever? What is really at the core of this argument for me? By asking these questions and being open to feeling what they bring up rather than trying to figure anything out intellectually we see further into the nature of what we are struggling with.

The final aspect of RAIN is ***non-identification***. After we have observed our experience with mindfulness, we illuminate that our thoughts, feelings, ideas, beliefs and trauma are not really who we are. We see this directly because in mindfulness we see that these things are impermanent, they constantly change, they come and go. However, what always remains is awareness or the deeper aspect of our consciousness, and it is untouched by what we experience, it merely reflects whatever is there. It is like a diamond in muddy water, it may be covered with mud, but when we clean it off, the diamond is still pure and unaffected. When we experience this awareness, we no longer need to identify with our thoughts and beliefs, mind states and feelings as who we are. This results in incredible freedom, because we are no longer so caught up in all the drama that we suffer so much from, and we can allow it to unfold without resistance or attachment. It also frees us to more deeply experience and appreciate life and whatever is happening, because we don't need it to be a certain way to support who we think we are.

Once you have some familiarity with the process of RAIN, it is fairly easy to apply in the moment when needed. Let's look at an example. Suppose you have an argument with your partner and you notice yourself becoming angry. You ***recognize*** that you are feeling an escalating anger and the discussion has turned into an argument, so you decide to pause and ask for some space. You go into the next room and sit and breath for a moment and allow yourself to ***accept*** what is happening. By accepting it you open the door to working with it in a healing way and you take responsibility for how you are feeling. As you continue to sit and ***investigate***, you become aware of a knot in your stomach and with further attention that is felt as anxiety. As you focus on the feeling of anxiety you experience it turn to fear, and you realize your initial anger in the argument came from a deep fear of losing your partner. With this fear you see a story in your mind that involves your partner leaving you, and all the details that go along with it, and its a familiar story. You realize this has been an ongoing pattern beginning in childhood when your father left. Having paused and approached this situation with mindfulness you have awakened the natural awareness within you, so you can see that this anger, fear and insecurity are not truly who you are, and you no longer need to ***identify*** with it as you were doing in the argument. The question may arise, "*What was I really protecting with my anger in the argument with my partner?*" You are able to experience it fully, release the pent up feeling, see into its nature and let go. When you cease to identify with a painful pattern or state of mind, you reclaim your power from it and are no longer under its control.

This is the process of healing with RAIN, and we can use it with practice to unravel long-term patterns and emotional blockages resulting in much greater freedom, joy and health. Mindfulness is a simple age-old technique that is always available to us in each moment.

The Warrior Archetype and the Reemergence of the Goddess

For the past few thousand years we have lived in a *patriarchal paradigm* where the masculine has been overemphasized at the expense of the feminine. This has produced not only the oppression of women, constant war and violence, but also inner conflict for both men and women as each struggles to be whole human being in a world where an imbalanced ideal is cherished. The overemphasis on the masculine has resulted in it taking a negative form as the feminine is devalued and even systematically repressed. This negative masculine form is cut off from its feminine side, and so is out of balance, and taken to an extreme in a futile attempt to compensate for the lack of grounding in the feminine.

This is symbolized by two archetypal patterns, in particular, that of the Negative Father and the Warrior. The Negative Father is the authoritarian head of the household who rules the family and is often the source of abuse, sexual misconduct and control. This pattern is also seen in the authoritarian governments that have become the norm where the government represents the ultimate controlling punitive father figure for its citizens. This isn't to say all fathers fall into this pattern, but it is symbolic of a key aspect of patriarchal power. As a counselor, I see many clients who have a figure in their lives in the role of the Negative Father, and much of their work in counseling involves working through trauma associated with that, as well as reclaiming their power from that figure, and this includes men and women.

Another key pattern in the patriarchal paradigm is the Warrior archetype. This pattern in its negative form represents the aggressive acting out of the masculine through war and domination. The Warrior is not an inherently negative symbol, but when it is not grounded in a healthy feminine center it becomes overly aggressive and indiscriminately violent. The Negative Warrior is an attempt at unity and wholeness, but because it attempts this through external conquest, it can never accomplish the desired wholeness and security. What is missing internally is projected externally and then aggressively pursued, so you get unending and escalating violence and war as the frustrated Warrior can never achieve peace and completeness.

The pattern of the Negative Warrior is especially important in the United States, where it has become a sacred symbol, in my opinion. The U.S. has entered a phase where it is actively engaging in unending war and the attempt to dominate other parts of the world through its unique status as the primary superpower. In America today the symbol of the Warrior is held so sacred that one cannot criticize war or those engaged in it without being labeled unpatriotic or at worst a traitor. Respectful open debate, something that is essential in a democracy, is often not tolerated without it degenerating into attacks. In my view, this is due to an extremely insecure attachment to the Warrior ideal with an underlying denial of the disconnection from the Divine Feminine.

America is certainly not the only country where this is playing out, but it seems to be taking an especially polarized and intense form here. We can see this in our continued wars fighting an obscure and all encompassing enemy, which is sometimes referred to as terror itself, the war on *terror* rather than *terrorism*. That would constitute a *war on an emotional state*, which is quite revealing in the sense that it is indeed terror that we project out externally and attempt to eradicate rather than facing within, where real healing is possible. Terror could be said to be the result of human beings living an incomplete existence, disconnected from key parts of themselves and their world (the natural world), the world becomes a terrifying place where what is unknown is feared and fought against rather than seen to be the mystery that it could be.

It is my view that today we find ourselves at the end of this dysfunctional world view, which is partially why we see it expressed in such extreme forms. *The patriarchal systems are breaking down, and as they do we see more desperate and intense reactions by forces trying to preserve them.* This is inevitable as well as futile, because the dissolution process is irreversible as the very power of the system becomes the force of its destruction. As difficult as this may be for many of us, it represents a very real potential for lasting change and *evolution of consciousness*, and I see this most represented by a reemergence of the Divine Feminine and the Goddess archetype. Essentially, the energies, which have been most repressed, are reasserting themselves as a natural process of balancing.

One of the most powerful manifestations of the Goddess is in the reaction of the Earth to the devastation that has been brought upon it by the patriarchal societies that relate to Mother Earth as a commodity to be possessed and used. Mother Earth is now responding with ever more forceful feedback in the forms of climate change, storms, earthquakes and other natural phenomena.

At the same time we are seeing the Goddess reassert herself in other more benign forms such as women stepping into more roles of leadership and authority as well as the powerful and increasing influence of Goddess-based and nature-based spirituality. The increasing popularity of neo-pagan spiritual paths is an example of this. Many of these groups involve women in positions of religious power and authority as well as an emphasis on the Divine Feminine and Mother Nature. However, this most often is not done at the expense of the masculine; for example, in Wicca, the Goddess and the God are honored together as two poles of the divine (in most Wiccan traditions). The rapidly growing interest in shamanism is another example of this, as people begin to reconnect with native cultures and more tribal alternative lifestyles. We also see a growing interest in plant medicine and more of a mainstreaming of alternative healing methods.

On an internal level, I'm seeing more and more men waking up to their deeper emotions and realizing that it is OK and even healthy to express emotions other than anger. I'm speaking here of men specifically, being a man myself and experiencing this, as well as the fact that many female writers have more effectively expressed what the reemergence of the Goddess means for women. In embracing the Divine Feminine within and beginning to see it as a powerful source of inspiration, healing and wholeness men can transform their expression of the masculine into its positive form, which is assertive rather than aggressive, and in service of the whole rather than destructive. The reintegration of the feminine side means that men can become whole human beings and also transform their relationship with women no longer projecting their feminine side onto women and then trying to possess and control them to reclaim it. Men can see women as their divine partners and as manifestations of the Goddess which brings great respect and a love that is unconditional.

We have a powerful opportunity to come back into balance as a planet, to reintegrate the cut off parts of ourselves and to heal ourselves and the planet as we step into a new dimension of consciousness. Resisting this time of change is what will bring us suffering and destruction, but we each have a choice as to how we proceed into the new paradigm. Hopefully, we will see this choice and choose well.

Survival

Now that I have left my job and chosen to pursue my heart path I am yet again directly up against the edge. One thing I always find at this edge is the fear of not being able to survive. Letting go of the world of career and work immediately brings up the fear that without that paycheck I won't be able to survive, to eat, to have shelter and clothing, etc. It's ironic that making a choice to follow the heart leads to a question of survival, but it shows how deeply ingrained the beliefs about security and material needs are in our society. In the old paradigm, following the heart and living in the moment is not taught to be a way to responsibly and effectively live life. Instead we are taught that we must sacrifice, struggle and make money if we want to have what we need and be OK in life, often at the expense of the heart and perhaps even our health and relationships.

If one chooses to step out of this crazy and dysfunctional perspective, the first things to be dealt with are the underlying beliefs from years of conditioning into this way of relating to livelihood. For me this has involved fear – no, let's say *terror* – that I won't make it, that I won't survive. In uncovering these beliefs and fears it has also illuminated the degree to which the old paradigm projects well-being and survival externally. We need to struggle to "find" a job, "make" money and "pursue" happiness, as if they are things we need from out there to be OK. This viewpoint is firmly fixed in materialism and completely discounts the idea that *we create our reality*, that external reality is a reflection of what we think, believe and feel inside. Trust in the heart, in the universe and abundance is sorely lacking. But that's to be expected, because who but a fortunate few are taught from childhood to openly feel life, to live in the present, to follow their intuition and believe in their creative power. For the rest of us it's a practice of illuminating and dissolving these conditioned beliefs, feeling and releasing the emotional trauma we carry from living in lack and separation, and learning to trust ourselves again and actively use our creative power not just in accepted artistic realms but in creatively dreaming up our lives. Life itself becomes the canvas.

I find that I'm compelled from a deep place to let these old ways go and realize a new way of living and being. Every time I try to do things the old way and work at an incongruent job so I can "make it", I find frustration, dissatisfaction and suffering. Living in a new way for me involves living in the moment and trusting in the universe. It involves being grateful for what I have and consciously putting my attention onto what I wish to create while seeing, believing and feeling its reality right now. It involves acceptance and surrender to what is, while allowing space to feel painful emotions, but not grasping onto them so they can flow and dissolve. This is not an easy practice, but an essential one, and one that I see almost everyone around me working on in their own way. I have a deep knowing that each of us is complete and has all the power we need to create everything necessary to live a joyous fulfilled life if we can only transcend the old patterns.

It's a work in progress and a wonderful, if sometimes terrifying, adventure. I not only want this for myself but for everyone, because it's painful to see people sacrificing their hearts; the pain underneath their expressions touches my heart.

Published in issue 6 of The Dot Connector magazine (November-December 2009).

Playthings of the gods

Walter C. Vetsch

For those of you who live on the surface of the Earth, you need to know that you do not live under the rule of any type of "government." You live under a cult. You cannot join this cult or even meet its members, because they are all safely hidden underground. This cult controls your life, and it controls your life to your detriment. If you expect any relief from your situation in the future, you must at the very least become aware of the true nature of your situation. Otherwise, those of you who cannot leave the planet Earth,will continue to be "playthings of the gods."

Developmental Example

Let's say you live in a village. In this village, the only source of water is the community well. However, the well is going dry and your fellow villagers are quite concerned. Now, let's say that one day you go out for a walk and you decide to go climb a hill that, for whatever reason, no one has ever climbed before. On the other side of the hill you find a natural spring with pure clean water, more than your village could ever want.

Now, we want to look at two possible scenarios for how you could handle this discovery. One scenario we will call "The Natural Way" and the second scenario we will call "The American Way."

The Natural Way

In this scenario, you scoop up some water and go back to the village and call all the people and tell them, *"Our water problems are solved! Just over that hill is a natural spring with more water than we will ever need, and it even tastes better than the water from the old well. Here, I brought some back. Try it!"* Everyone is thrilled and you begin to discuss some plan to maybe make some pipe, or something, so that you will not need to climb the hill to get the water, and stuff like that. This is the "Natural Way."

The American Way

In this scenario, you scoop up some water and go back to the village and call the people and tell them, "*Look what I have here – fresh clean water. Try some.*" And they are all happy and ask, "*Where is the water, so we can use it to save our village?*" But then you say, "*That information is classified and a trade secret. What I gave you was a free sample. However, I am now 'the water company,' and if you want water so you can continue to live, you must pay me, in advance.*"

So, now the people of the village are giving you money. With that money you can hire some of the people to go get water and bring it back for the desperate villagers.

However, your "trade secret" is fragile because, if anyone learns about the spring on the other side of the hill, the people will go get their water for free and you will be out of business, and that may well be the least of your trouble. So, you must carefully choose people for your "company" and make sure they are sworn to secrecy. You can offer your faithful employees incentives to keep quiet, like free water for them and their families, and even extra water just to waste.

As your profits increase, you can afford to spend more money on security. First, you will want to use psychological techniques to make sure that no regular people from the village ever get the notion to climb the hill. You will want to start rumors that some monster lives on the other side of the hill and that anyone who goes there will be gobbled up and never return. Now, just in case someone does not believe you, you will need to hire some snipers to hide close to the top of the hill. If anyone looks like they are getting close to discovering your "trade secret," the snipers are to kill them and throw them in a hole on the other side of the hill – people will be told "the monster must have got them."

As time goes on and your profits grow, now that you have more money than you will ever need, you look to other neat things you can do. With your money, you can take over the press and the education system. People will be instructed that you are now "the god of water" and that you have always existed and see all and know all, etc. The schoolbooks will be rewritten so that kids will be taught this. If you encounter dissent, well, there is always the hole on the other side of the hill and the "monster story" to explain disappearances.

You can also now afford to do nice things every once and a while to make people like you, such as giving free water to starving poor people who can't afford to pay you – but just enough to barely keep them alive.

Also, you may want to consider your faithful employees. Of course, you will have trained security people to watch them and make sure they remain faithful. However, a better way to cultivate loyalty is with special perks others do not have. In the village, water is precious to the desperate people, because they do not know the truth. However, you could not care less about water, because you have more than you will ever need. So why not be totally decadent? You can construct a "recreation center" for your employees, with a swimming pool and spa, so that they can have fun and waste all the water they want. Later you can expand this to a "secret village" located on your side of the hill, where those loyal to you will enjoy every luxury while the regular people in the original village will suffer and beg for mercy as you consistently raise the price of your water.

This is the "American Way."

Seed Knowledge

Today's young people have no trouble at all accepting a world filled with technology such as communications satellites and instant communication from anywhere to anywhere with a tiny cell phone. However, all of this stuff is very, very recent history. If you look back in history, does it not strike you as strange that the people of Earth went from riding horses and reading by candles or kerosene lanterns to our current world of going on trips to the moon and being surrounded by every conceivable type of electronic gadget in less than one generation? From the perspective of history, this is very strange. Look at the length of time other evolutionary learning processes took. Nothing like this has ever happened before. So, common sense should tell you that there is a missing part to this story – something that would explain this unprecedented jump in technical evolution.

A chance

In the early 1940s, a decision was made to "take a chance" with the people of Earth and to provide them with certain "seed knowledge" that they could use to raise their developmental level to a point where they would become an entrance level advanced civilization and be able to interact with other advanced civilizations from other parts of the physical universe. Essentially every technology we enjoy today was derived in some way from this seed knowledge.

So, representatives came to Earth to deliver the seed knowledge and discuss the potential and future evolution of the people of the Earth.

Agreements

The seed knowledge was not free. In order to obtain it, the representatives of Earth had to agree that the knowledge was to be used for the benefit of all the people of the Earth to promote their positive evolution and development. The Earth representatives were made aware that the seed knowledge did have a potential for abuse. They were required to promise not to do this, and they were also warned that there would be penalties if the knowledge was used in any manner other than the positive and constructive manner they had agreed. It was explained to the representatives of Earth that violations of this agreement would result in punishments and sanctions and could possibly make it necessary for the providers of the knowledge to correct their mistake by destroying the planet Earth to protect the peace of the Universe and comply with Universal Laws.

Prohibitions against nuclear devices

It was also explained to the Earth representatives, as they progressed, that nuclear detonations cause disruptions in space-time, which can be detected by any advanced civilization and traced back to their source planet. They are considered bad form and should not be done. Unfortunately, Earth scientists got interested in the time distortion side effect of a nuclear detonation and, trying to get the secrets of time, kept blowing up bombs until they figured it out and then quickly got a world ban on new explosions in order to keep others from learning what they had.

Status

Obviously, Earth has not become the global advanced civilization that was intended. In fact, the Earth representatives chose to break all of their agreements and use the seed knowledge to set up a global dictatorship, which is commonly called the New World Order. If they had kept their agreement, the general population of Earth would not know poverty or disease and would be free to travel and visit other advanced civilizations throughout the universe by this point in time. This was the hope and intent when the seed knowledge was handed over. However, as with any gamble, sometimes you do not get what you want despite your best efforts.

Compartmentalization

Compartmentalization is a method of information control designed to create groups of people in varying degrees of intellectually challenged states. It is a mind control system,which allows a set of bosses (who designed the system and so are allowed to know everything) to control the remainder of the population by allowing them to know only what they "need to know" to do their respective slave jobs to serve the ruling bosses.

History

There were similar systems of control long before modern government-sponsored compartmentalization came into existence. Adam Weishaupt, founder of the Illuminati, designed a system of levels (with himself as the boss, of course) and is quoted as giving out instructions to his "higher" followers for recruitment of "lower" followers as follows:

"These good folk swell our numbers and fill our money box. Set yourselves to work; these gentlemen must be made to nibble at the bait... But this sort of people must always be made to believe that the grade they have reached is the last."

This basic model is common to modern government-sponsored compartmentalization systems, as well as those used by various religions, cults, and secret societies.

All of these groups obtain their energy – usually in the form of money – from the lower levels of the group, who are generally good and well-meaning people who have no idea what the leadership is doing with their money, but assume it must be something good. Churches and cults scare money out of their followers with threats about punishment in the "afterlife." Governments, of course, just order people to pay taxes and deal with them by force if they refuse. However, in all cases, money is extracted from the lower levels and sent to the higher levels so that the people in the higher levels can have every luxury they want at the expense of the lower levels.

In the U.S. system, ordinary people have no idea that everything they do is, directly or indirectly, for the benefit of the group we call "gods." They do not know that this group exists.

Huxley's classic book, *Brave New World*, describes a system of population control where most people are chemically damaged to make them suitable for some level of slavery. The master class consists of people who are not damaged, i.e., people who are allowed to develop unique personalities and have independent thought. They are equivalent to the "gods" in the New World Order model.

The people in our model, who are "below the gods," do not have to be grown in test tubes and damaged with chemicals, as they are in Huxley's novel, to be functional slaves – they simply have to be given an inferior education. This works just as well. We even publicly recognize this when we use terms such as "blue collar" and "white collar" to separate classes, or "casts," of people based upon level of education.

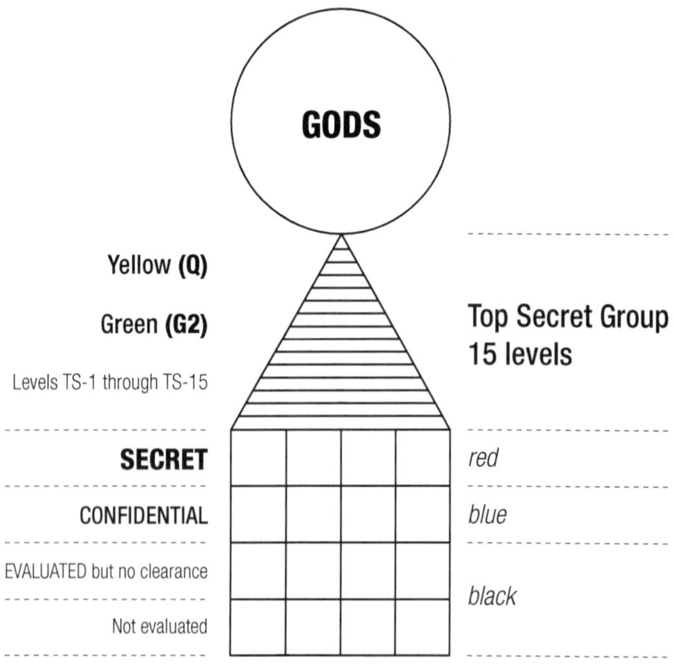

New World Order compartmentalization model.

The major levels

The major levels of the system are: *(1)* the gods, *(2)* the Top Secret Group, and *(3)* the Compartment Group. Basically, the Compartment Group "houses" the general population who do the general jobs needed to maintain social infrastructure.

The Top Secret Group consists of "executive level slaves" who control the Compartment Group. Most people in the Compartment Group do not know that the Top Secret Group exists.

At the top we have the group of "gods." They live free of all controls and are allowed to know all available knowledge and are provided with every conceivable luxury. Their existence is generally unknown to the two lower groups.

The Compartment Group

The Compartment Group is symbolized by the crosshatch pattern to represent the "intellectual boxes" in which these people live. They probably do not realize that they live in an "information cage" from which they cannot escape. As stated by Adam Weishaupt, they are conditioned to believe that *"the grade they have reached is the last."* They are happy because they do not know anything better exists.

Most people in the Compartment Group are so stupid that there is no reason for the government to pay any attention to them. Therefore, they are not even looked at and form the "not evaluated" level.

Above them is the level of people who may have some capacity for independent thought who must be "checked out." If hired to do something related to government, they are coded "black" for "no security clearance," but they have been checked out to make sure they are no threat.

The two levels above this are Confidential and Secret. The color code used on government ID badges is blue for Confidential and red for Secret clearance. Confidential and Secret clearances involve information that is "temporary." For example, the combination to a safe may be a secret but it is not permanent – if you leave your job, the combination can be changed and you will no longer know it. Therefore, as a function of time, you are gradually "relieved" of your secrecy oath simply because the secrets you once knew no longer exist. Certain secret codes also change periodically, and so you are only bound by your secrecy oath while the codes you know are current.

The Top Secret Group

The fundamental difference between the Compartment Group and the Top Secret Group is the permanence of the information. Top Secrets generally get information, which the government never intends the general population to ever know. Consequently, Top Secret clearances require an oath that the person will "never leave the service of the government" and will be bound by his oath of secrecy for life.

Examples of knowledge and events that you would never be allowed to talk freely about would be contact with aliens, time travel, information about other planets (detailed information like you would have if you were actually there), the underground cities and installations, and anything about the "gods."

Even though people in the Top Secret Group must take the most serious oath of secrecy, they do not necessarily know all that much. There are 15 levels of Top Secret and, following the Weishaupt model, people in the Top Secret Group are conditioned to believe that whatever level they are (TS1 – TS15) is the highest level there is.

For example, if you interview a person with a security clearance and ask, "*Do you have a security clearance?*", they are trained to say, "*Yes.*" But, when you ask, "*What level?*", they are trained to answer, "*The best.*" This is because they believe that whatever they have is "the best." So, now you have to guess the level. You may say, "*Is it Q?*" If you guess the correct level, they are supposed to confirm it. This is the little game you play when making a new contact.

In the Top Secret Group there are mainly intelligence people like G2, MI6 and the like, and others, whose job – like scientists – is not an intelligence work. Intelligence uses a green stripe on their ID badges, and Q uses a yellow stripe.

CODE WORD CLEARANCES. In addition to the main 15 levels, there are special clearances called "*Code Word Clearances.*" These clearances create special working groups in unique areas, whose members share a set of "code words" to communicate information to each other. People in different "code word groups" would have a different set of words common to that group, which would not be recognized by other groups.

By example, a friend of mine knew a famous doctor. He had won awards and international recognition for his research on the eye, using dogs for destructive testing. My friend saw him at a party and, it so happened, she had a sick dog with some kind of eye trouble. She approached the man and asked his advice, since he was so famous for his dog research. She was speechless when he replied, *"Dogs? I don't know anything about dogs. We don't use dogs. We use niggers. Niggers are better than dogs."*

"Dogs" was a code word for black people. In this way the doctor was able to "operate in plain sight" and even receive public awards for his research. Of course, people with code word clearance knew what "dogs" really meant, and what was really going on, but the general public was clueless. This is how code word clearance works in everyday life.

The gods

The gods are the main subject of this book, and we will get into much greater detail about them later. At the present,we want to go over some misconceptions you may have when you look at the schematic model for compartmentalization.

Although there is a progression from the bottom to the top, where we label "gods," this system is not a "social ladder" that you can climb if you have persistence. This is a control system. It is designed to keep you where you are. It is not designed to encourage you to progress and reward you with higher status for your good efforts.

The gods are not people who were once ordinary people. Most of them are from ruling bloodlines, who in the past considered themselves to have "the divine right of kings" by virtue of birth into certain families. They have always contemplated making the Earth into a global dictatorship. When they learned of the "seed knowledge," they set about creating a scheme to violate the agreements and use the knowledge for their personal benefit and for world domination in violation of the Universal Laws. Although there are exceptions, in general, you cannot buy your way into this group with money or anything else.

Membership is a birthright. You must be born into a family of gods to become a god. Nothing else matters.

The gods are equal among themselves. They are above "security clearances" and knowledge control and are allowed to know all that is currently available to know.

They live "above the game" which they created and are the "game masters" watching the general population fumble around in the maze (or matrix) they created for their personal needs and enjoyment.

"Comfortable Clothes" is the general code word for these people. When you *"agree to put on the comfortable clothes,"* you leave the general population of the Earth forever and enter the special world of the gods. There is no return from this.

Belief Systems

Belief systems are sort of fairy tales that are used as a substitute for reality, when: *(1)* reality is not known, or *(2)* reality is preferred not to be known. Although a belief system may be a logical construct, it is not necessarily true. Truth has no relationship to logic. Logical constructs can be designed to prove anything. The classic example is the science, which "proves" that a bumble bee cannot possibly fly. Clearly, the bumble bee lives in a different belief system, because it seems to have no trouble at all flying around.

Essentially all the population of Earth lives under one or more of many belief systems.

The Catholic Belief System

The Catholic belief system is a good religious example, because there is documentation available on them and their exploits have recently become popular with the press and the U.S. court system. Let's take a look at this belief system.

The sex sub-system

We may as well begin with the sex sub-system, since that is what Catholic Priests have become known for in recent history. To understand the sex subsystem, first realize that the Catholic Church is simply a continuation of the Roman Empire. When it was realized that the Roman Empire could not take over the world by military power, it converted itself into the Catholic Church and set about taking over the world by scaring people into obeying it with its special take on religious truth. This approach has been quite successful, although the church must share power with other religions using similar methods.

Now, in the Roman Empire, there was a belief system concerning men and women. In this belief system, women were considered a secondary creation and therefore inferior to men. Consequently, it was considered wrong to have sex with a woman for fun, because she was an inferior being like a dog or a goat or whatever.

Therefore, when a man wanted sex for fun, he should choose his equal for his partner, i.e., another man. And, just like men today prefer young women, the Roman men preferred young boys for sex partners. This was considered the correct way to do things at that time. Sex with the inferior women was considered occasionally necessary, so she could make more people to keep society going. Women generally stayed pregnant from about 12 years old until they died or lived long enough to reach menopause (rare).

Today, there is a legal problem with this belief system, because our society considers raping young boys to be a crime. However, the Catholic Priesthood does not live under the rules of the modern world. They live under the rules of the Roman Empire. And their activities are protected by church secrecy. Their very way of life depends on following their ancient beliefs and rituals, and to change it would spell the end to their collective identity as priests.

Therefore, no matter how much trouble they get into for raping children, they are going to continue to find a way to do it. They will just get better at keeping it a secret from outsiders. In the past, they were protected by an "aura of goodness," which presumed that a priest could do no wrong. Since that is shattered now, more direct methods will need to be employed so that they can continue "business as usual."

Incidentally, many "primitive" cultures operating in the world today still use the belief system about women being a secondary creation and therefore inferior to men. It is really only in the United States that the women's liberation idea has taken hold.

Blind faith sub-system

Until relatively recently in Catholic history, sermons were given in Latin. This is really weird. The "bell rings," and you report to church to hear some priest talk for an hour or so in a language you can't understand, and then you turn over 10% of your money to him as payment for his "service." What did you learn to enhance your spiritual advancement by listening to Latin for one hour? Why is this worth 10% of your money? Well, you do not consider these questions because this is a belief system and a belief system is based on raw belief and nothing else. You are not supposed to question your belief.

Recent Pope history

The Catholic Church periodically elects a "god," which it calls the Pope. The last Pope was John Paul II. When John Paul was a young man, he worked for a chemical company. He was the salesman who sold the cyanide to Hitler for the gas chambers. (For documentation please see *Behold A Pale Horse* by William Cooper.) Now we step ahead to Pope Benedict. He is not just someone who helped the Nazis – he is a real Nazi. He joined the Hitler Youth at age 14 or so, as reported by the national news. Of course, both of these "good men" were duly elected as "gods," and now they want to hurry up and make John Paul a "saint."

By what stretch of the imagination do we conclude that there is anything remotely spiritual or "godly" about a guy who sold Hitler his poison gas chemicals or his Nazi successor from the Hitler Youth group? It is said that Benedict is "strong defender of the faith." I guess he is. He's a Nazi. Remember, "master race," "rightful rulers of the world," etc. Come on!

Catholic level of spirituality

We are going to talk a bit about Spirituality – legitimate Spirituality – because it is very real and important to all souls. Just because most churches are run by assorted quacks, nuts and weirdos does not mean that the for real GOD does not exist or that we should not seek Spiritual Enlightenment. It is important to seek Spirituality. It is your duty as a Human Being to do this. Animals do not have this inclination or ability, but you do, and to make best use of it is the true purpose of human existence.

Having cleared that up, let's look and see what, if any, Spiritual goodies the Catholic Church has to offer.

The diagram on the right is the Catholic schematic model for its "path to heaven." The vertical line represents the path and the semicircle to the right at the top represents the end of the path. The "X" is a symbol used for a gate. Since there is only one gate in the model, this is a path to some location on the right (good) side of the astral plane. So, this is a psychic path. It is not spiritual. To reach the spiritual realm you need to go through at least two more gates – to the causal and then to the mental-etheric plane. After that, you must cross a barrier (which usually requires a competent guide) to get into the spiritual zone. So, there is nothing great about this path. Once you die, you ***must*** go to some astral plane because there is no other place you can go to (unless you are spiritually advanced and can get above the astral plane somewhere). Even dead people who are earthbound running around graveyards or haunting houses are technically on the first astral sub-plane. So getting to "somewhere" on the astral plane is automatic for most people, even if they have no type of religious training at all.

The astral plane contains about 100 sub-planes, and these sub-planes also have sub-planes. These are sometimes called "groves." When you spend your life in some belief system that conditions you to believe that "heaven is like this," the force of the group imagination creates such a place somewhere on the astral plane. When you die, you go there and your desires are fulfilled. All garden-variety religions have such a place on the astral plane. The concept of "groves," or compartments, means that they never meet each other. Baptists would gather and believe that "they made it to heaven," but the "other religions" must have been false and those people must be burning in hell because they are not there with them. But the other groups ***are*** there, in their own little "grove," and they feel the same way – that they "made it" and the others did not. Since you can instantly create your desires with imagination on this plane, most souls are convinced that they are happily in heaven forever. Eventually, the time comes when their "heavenly buddies" can't find them. This is because they have reincarnated and must now "do it all again" and hopefully make a more realistic choice in how to find true spirituality. Those who achieve this do not have to return to the physical creation.

So, basically, you would probably be much better off if you just led a decent life and never heard of the Catholic belief system, because you would not be conflicted with all of their out of date teachings, not to mention the trauma of possibly being raped as a kid. You would most likely reach a higher level after death without their "help."

Cults and Psychiatric Groups

Cults are "custom made" belief systems that are generally designed to indoctrinate followers with some seemingly logical construct that makes them want to stay with the cult and obey and follow the leader. A certain level of skill is required to be a successful cult leader, because you cannot force people to stay with you – you must somehow convince them that they need you or scare them somehow into not leaving you. Of course, you will want money and services from the followers.

Psychiatric groups are generally sponsored by governments. Therefore, they do not need to con people into following them. They have the authority to force people to obey them and to brainwash them into obedience with mind control drugs. Although the general psychiatric language remains the same throughout the world, how it is interpreted does not. For example, a young girl in Saudi would be considered abnormal if she wanted a Barbie doll, but a young girl in America would be considered abnormal if she ***did not*** want a Barbie doll. The old Soviet Union loved psychiatry, because it could call anyone who did not "love the party" abnormal and then torture them until they changed their mind as "treatment" for their "illness."

One main hallmark of cults is some scheme to control sex. If you can control someone's sex desire, you can control that person. Therefore, it will be found that cults have worked up some belief system saying that followers should give up sex. Psychiatrists simply use drugs to make people under their control incapable of having or enjoying sex.

An interesting recent development in the United States is the attempt to use this classic cult technique on the general population by threatening them with death if they have sex. Now that the U.S. government has successfully spread the AIDS virus that it developed and manufactured at Fort Detrick, MD, around the world, it can argue that "if you sleep around you will surely die," and so you "should be celibate if you want to live." This argument is straight out of "How to make a cult 101." Of course, all the "important people" have been vaccinated with the antidote to AIDS, so they are free to have all the sex they want with no worry. Visions of the "Junior Anti-Sex League" from *1984* – you can't have it, but the "inner party" members can.

Belief Systems Based on Genetics

Genetic based belief systems argue that a certain group with a common genetic trait is "special" and apart from "ordinary people" who do not share this specific genetic sub-code. Let's look at some examples.

Hitler's system

Hitler's system argued that blue eyed blondes were the "master race" and should rightfully rule the world. Although, mainly due to the concept of political correctness, since the U.S. champions integration and race equality, people look down on Hitler's argument that blue eyed blondes were somehow superior, it should be noted that the United States used the same genetic selection system when it was fighting Hitler. If you go back and find some color pictures of men in the U.S. Navy during the late 1940s to early 1950s, you will find that they are ***all*** blue-eyed blondes. And they are not just blue eyed, but are the special "azure blue," which sort of shines as if it was lit up.

There are no exceptions. People do not seem to realize that the different U.S. armed forces were populated with specific genetic types before the services were ordered integrated. The Air Force also liked the Hitler model SS genetics (incidentally, the "SS" is a schematic symbol for the double helix of the DNA molecule). The Army was for the "lower genetic classes," which means brown eyes and not necessarily white skin.

The Jewish system

When the bodies we use on this planet were being manufactured, the different races were created for different specialties. The Jewish race was programmed with a predisposition for administrative jobs like accounting, working with money, and so on. Somehow, as time passed, this became interpreted to mean that "god" (by which is apparently meant the genetic engineers from the Orion Empire who wrote the codes and made original people) "gave the world to them."

Hitler knew about this special sub-code and, since he had decided that his chosen genetic type should rightfully rule the world, obviously he wanted to make the competition extinct. It is because of this belief system that Jews are taught to breed within their race and so preserve the special sub-code. It is also why they do not actively seek to convert people to their religion. You cannot "make someone a Jew," because they must be born with this sub-code in order to be really a Jew.

Sub-codes in the ruling bloodlines of the world

The ruling families, or ruling bloodlines, of the world also seek to inbreed to preserve special genetic sub-codes, which they feel make them special or give them special powers that others do not have. It is essentially impossible to rise beyond a point in the power structure of the world without coming from one of these special ruling bloodlines. You could call it a sort of "genetic glass ceiling." The ruling bloodlines are above it, and the rest of humanity is below it, and there is no inclination to change things.

By example, in the [2004] election for U.S. President, George Bush and John Kerry were cousins. They were from the same bloodline. It did not matter who you voted for – either way, that bloodline would rule. It is very doubtful that Bush and Kerry did not know they were cousins. They are probably fast friends and meet at "family reunions." If U.S. news people were watching some other country, where the only two people running for leader were some guy and his cousin, you can bet they would be crying about how this was not legitimate and fair, and so on. But the press knows how to behave have themselves when talking about this country, and so you never heard a peep about this fact, and you probably did not know it until just now!

Effect of genetic engineering on the sub-code concept

In the past, the only way to duplicate a genetic trait was to mate in the usual way with an appropriate person. However, with nanotechnology, scientists can sit down and hand-assemble a molecule, which means that they can hand-assemble a DNA molecule and write any code into it that they want. This sort of "cheapens" the concept that you are somehow of great value because you are from some special bloodline, since the codes that are supposed to make you so special can now be made in the lab. Also, by tinkering, you might manufacture a new person with some revolutionary special power or special predisposition. The alien genetic engineers had no trouble doing that tens of thousands of years ago, and we now have or will soon have the equivalent abilities. So, this puts a whole new slant on the "superior by reason of genetics" concept.

The U.S. Monetary System

Not very long ago, U.S. money was "real," because it was backed up by gold. Now U.S. currency is called "fiat," which means "faith based imaginary currency." It has value only because people believe it has value. It is purely and simply a belief system that gives value to the various pieces of paper that the government prints.

As long as everyone accepts the money belief system, it works just as well as the real system based on a real substance (gold) as opposed to imagination. However, should it occur to people to ask, "*Where's the beef?*", they would find themselves with hands full of worthless paper, because there is no "beef."

Obviously, faith is harder to maintain than hard reality. Someone would be hard pressed to accept the argument that a block of gold was worthless crap. However, should someone argue that U.S. currency is worthless crap, it would be hard to logically argue against them, since it is imaginary and has nothing backing it but blind faith. In order to stabilize this belief system, it is important that people be conditioned to "just not ask" but "accept on faith" that "everything is fine." Consequently, anyone who tried to "undermine the faith" would be a threat to the nation and would have to be quickly dealt with to "preserve the faith."

The plan to convert from real currency to imaginary currency appears to be inherently sinister as supported by the following quote. Edward Mandell House had this to say in a private meeting with Woodrow Wilson (President, 1913-1921):

"[Very] soon, every American will be required to register their biological property in a national system designed to keep track of the people, and that will operate under the ancient system of pledging. By such methodology, we can compel people to submit to our agenda, which will affect our security as a chargeback for our fiat paper currency. Every American will be forced to register or suffer being unable to work and earn a living. They will be our chattels, and we will hold the security interest over them forever by operation of the law merchant under the scheme of secured transactions. Americans, by unknowingly or unwittingly delivering the bills of lading to us, will be rendered bankrupt and insolvent, forever to remain economic slaves through taxation, secured by their pledges. They will be stripped of their rights and given a commercial value designed to make us a profit, and they will be none the wiser, for not one man in a million could ever figure our plans and, if by accident one or two should figure it out, we have in our arsenal plausible deniability.

After all, this is the only logical way to fund government, by floating liens and debt to the registrants in the form of benefits and privileges. This will inevitably reap to us huge profits beyond our wildest expectations and leave every American a contributor to this fraud, which we will call 'Social Insurance.' Without realizing it, every American will insure us for any loss we may incur, and in this manner every American will unknowingly be our servant, however begrudgingly. The people will become helpless and without any hope for their redemption, and we will employ the high office of the President of our dummy corporation to foment this plot against America."

Maintenance of Belief Systems

Once you have established a belief system, you must maintain it. There must be some method to constantly reinforce the belief or it will gradually weaken and fade away. There are various ways to do this. Also, there are static and dynamic belief systems.

Static systems, such as many church systems, cling on a set of beliefs from long ago, no matter how much the real world changes. Because of this, sometimes they die out of attrition. But some seem to hang on.

Dynamic belief systems, such as the U.S. consciousness belief system, are always changing. Today's belief is not the same as a past time belief. It is sort of like the *1984* model, where you are at war with one country and love the other one day and the reverse is true the next day. Incidentally, if you have not read this classic novel by George Orwell, you really should.

Using the U.S. belief system as an example, some principles completely reverse. By example, in the 1950s, the only people allowed to have knowledge of the female reproductive system were doctors. They were forbidden to tell women anything about how their body worked. Vice squad agents would send pregnant undercover officers to doctors and they would beg to be told how to avoid becoming pregnant again. If the doctor said anything, he was busted.

Today, we have the reverse. Grade school kids get sex-ed. The schools pass out condoms. There is an abortion clinic on almost every corner, and 25% of pregnant girls kill their babies.

In the U.S., the belief system is maintained by the daily mass media news. Every day there are five or six news stories that are used by everyone. You may find it strange that thousands of "independent" TV and radio stations and print media just happen to report the same set of stories every day. This "information fix" keeps you locked into the U.S. belief system for another day, until your next "news fix." It has been suggested that, if something went wrong with the mass media so that it stopped operating, the U.S. government would quickly lose control of the people and possibly would not be able to regain control. If mass media stopped, people would have to resort to independent thought to decide what to believe and what to do. Once they learned how to do this, it could be difficult to "recapture" them.

Belief Systems and Compartmentalization

Belief systems go hand in hand with compartmentalization. Belief systems create a compartment, and compartments created by compartmentalization develop internal belief systems.

Belief systems cause followers to voluntarily limit their life activities. Church systems teach followers that they are "chosen" and the rest of the world is not, so people limit their relationships to members of that specific system so as not to get "tainted by the non-believers." They may also have weird dietary and other obsessive-compulsive habits that they feel they must have to be "saved."

Government SCI (sensitive compartmentalized intelligence) groups may drift so far away from "normal reality" that the only people they can relate to are their coworkers. Remote viewers, for example, would have trouble relating to everyday people and getting them to understand the things they know, assuming they were allowed to talk about them (which they are not). Therefore, their only friends would be fellow members of their "belief system." Hopefully, the government trains some girls to be remote viewers, so the guy viewers would have a chance to have some type of normal home life. Otherwise, their uninitiated mate would eventually leave them.

Research and Development

Adolf Hitler – the Father of Human Destructive Testing

Destructive testing is the process of obtaining information about something, in which the "something" does not survive the test, but the needed information is obtained. For example, if you want to know how much weight a concrete beam will support, you keep putting weight on it until it breaks. This ruins the concrete beam, but it gives you the information that you can now use to assign specifications to equivalent concrete beams that are not broken, so that they will not break in use.

Human destructive testing means doing experiments on people that will kill these people, but will give you information you are seeking about humans, which you can then use to help (or maybe hurt) other humans that you predict will respond in a similar manner. You justify the killing of a few to advance medicine for the many.

It used to be unthinkable to do such a thing. Researchers were supposed to use lab rats and the like to get information. All this changed when Hitler started herding people into his camps. Since he was going to kill them anyway, the thought occurred to the German pharmaceutical companies to use these people as test animals instead of the usual lab rats.

One drug developed using human-destructive testing was a prescription face cream mainly used by women. It contains an acid and is used to create a smoother complexion by basically "eating away" a layer of skin. It is still used today. In the research, the drug company wanted to know how much acid to use in the formula. So, they made up batches with different concentrations and took them to one of Hitler's camps. Then they brought in the first set of test girls. Oops, too much acid, face came off. Throw them in the furnace and bring in the next set of girls. This went on until the right mix was obtained by trial and error. Many women use this cream today, and it is very doubtful that they know how the formula was perfected. Apparently, many other drugs and medical procedures were perfected using destructive testing on the people in the camps.

You won't see people on TV praising Hitler for his accomplishments in medicine, but it is a different story in private. I have been to private gatherings where doctors have nothing but praise Hitler for being the first to dare to use humans in experiments and how he advanced science with his experiments. They absolutely love the man. And after he "showed the way" to the fast track for the accumulation of medical knowledge, others got the word quickly.

Obviously, it is a crime to pick up people off the street and kill them to get medical knowledge. But there are ways around this. For one thing, essentially everything governments do is a state secret, so if they want to kill people, no one is going to find out. One case where this happened was the search for a "vaccine" against radiation. The elite wanted to make sure they would survive in case of a nuclear war. They developed the vaccine (which is secret and only available to the elite ruling class), but at the cost of killing over 100,000 U.S. citizens in secret experiments. The government has admitted to some radiation experiments, but has never discussed the vaccine project.

Perhaps the largest human destructive testing project was done in Vietnam during the "war." Actually, it was not a standard war, because the U.S. controlled both sides. It was more of a "war project" to take advantage of the fact that you can get away with stuff during a war that you cannot get away with under normal conditions. In Vietnam, anyone who had a medical research project they wanted to do simply built a facility, grabbed as many Vietnamese people as they needed for the experiments, and went to work. When the project was over, the research team packed up all their notes and data and left. The "test people" were left locked in their cages and then an air strike was called in to destroy all the evidence. Many such projects were done, which is why people in power wanted to keep the "war" going as long as possible.

It was during this period that human physical death was eliminated. Beyond the 1960s time frame no "important" person has died.

Overcoming Physical Death

Cloning

Cloning was discovered on a college campus in the time frame of the 1960s. It was so simple to do that kids were doing it at home. Immediately, there was talk about how this was somehow "not right" and should be stopped. But news travels fast between college campuses, and soon everyone knew about cloning. By the time government scientists realized the potential of what had been discovered, it was too late to recall the information, and the concept of cloning became public knowledge.

If cloning had been discovered today, you would never know about it. This is because there is a system in place to monitor college campuses just in case someone makes a significant discovery such as cloning. Today all the persons involved would be immediately seized by government agents, and all the research records would be confiscated. The people involved would be ordered to sign non-disclosure agreements. Anyone refusing would be killed.

As soon as government scientists heard about cloning, the first words out of their mouths were, "We're going to make people." They knew the power and potential of what they had, and they hoped that the general public would never figure it out.

Early tests were, of course, done with animals. One such test was with a dog. It so happened that this (dead) dog had been a show dog and knew all kinds of tricks that it performed on command. When the clone was made, the scientists found, to their surprise, that the clone dog responded to the dead dog's name and all of the commands to do tricks that the dead dog knew. It was at this point that all government cloning projects went "black." The secret of cloning had been discovered: a clone is not just something that looks like the original – it is the original complete with memories. This is the secret the government hopes you never learn. This is why the government wants a worldwide ban on cloning – so that ordinary people will never discover this truth and the process can be used for the elite as one of the methods to allow them to live physically forever.

The next step was to make people. The government guessed – and it proved true – that they could now "bring back to life" anyone who had died if they could find a DNA sample for that person. They "brought back" people like Einstein, Tesla, Edison, and the like. They also brought back people they secretly admired, like Adolf Hitler.

We need to get into some esoteric stuff at this point. Life continues beyond death. When someone loses access to their physical body, they find themselves in their astral, or "light," body. Most people in atheist, materialist countries such as the United States assume that nothing exists beyond physical death. When they die, they find themselves "earthbound" and really confused, because they can see people and hear people, but those people can't see or hear them. They do not know they are dead.

They continue to have a natural affinity for the specific vibratory pattern of the last physical body they had. Unfortunately, it cannot be reanimated because all the blood has been drained out and replaced with poison to make sure it can't reanimate. Before embalming, some people did come back to life only to find themselves locked in a box and buried. Since they could not get out, they eventually died "for real."

Anyway, there is a natural affinity to locate this particular genetic structure. So, if you are psychic and go wandering around a graveyard, you will find astral forms, who don't know they are dead, hanging around where their body is buried, trying to figure out why it does not work any more. Since you can communicate with them, you will probably explain to them that they are dead and that they need to move on (up) to where other beings like themselves live.

Let us suppose, however, that a perfectly good genetic structure exists (clone) which has the exact vibratory signature as the spirit's old body did, except that this one works. Well, the same natural affinity that led the spirit to the graveyard would now lead it to the clone, and the clone is in perfect health and can be reanimated. This is how you get people "back from the dead."

There has been assisting technology developed based on other secret discoveries in temporal science. Obviously, a clone begins as a single cell and it takes some time before it is a recognizable and viable structure. But, because of time acceleration technology, a "grown-up" clone can be whipped up rather quickly. This is most likely begun using an "artificial womb." The government already has a law prohibiting any ordinary person from attempting to build an artificial womb to make sure they do not catch on to this secret.

Cloning is only effective for spiritually immature entities who are earthbound due to desire. A spiritually mature person upon physical death would quickly leave this dimension of existence and could not be forced to come back by cloning or any other method. However, this is not a problem, because the type of person the government wants to bring back is filled with earthly desires for money, power and the like, and also is likely to be intrinsically evil. Such people cannot and also do not want to leave the earth, so it is no problem to "bring them back." The government has no use for legitimately good and spiritually developed people and considers them "a threat to its security."

Cloning is one of the most revolutionary discoveries of modern times. How many people the government is willing to kill, and how long it can keep it up to prevent this knowledge from becoming public, remains to be seen. It only takes one successful clone case to be made public to shatter the secrecy and make the knowledge and technology available to everyone. And the world is still a big place.

Controlled reincarnation

Controlled reincarnation devices take advantage of the fact that astral entities cannot escape from a charged Faraday cage. Basically, this is any space enclosed by a metal screen that is charged with electricity (high voltage) with respect to earth ground. You can make such a space any size you want as long as you have the material to build it and an uninterruptible supply of power to keep the cage charged. Obviously, governments have plenty of both.

You have now created a sort of "sub-space" of the universe. If you know what is inside this controlled space, you can cause nature to obey your will. For the purpose of controlled reincarnation, if someone dies inside this special space and someone else gets pregnant inside this space at roughly the same time, nature will reincarnate the dead person into the new fetus because that is its only option.

This technique has some problems because of the lag time of waiting for the new child to grow old enough to be told what happened and then trying to get the child to recall its past life.

Body swapping

Body swapping uses adult bodies and special equipment to strip the spirit out of one body and put it in the other and do the reverse at the same time. The advantage of this method is that you immediately get a useable body that is "ready to go." Controlled reincarnation sort of "cooperates with nature" and is not a Universal Law violation, however, stealing someone else's body is a violation. Clearly, governments really could not care less.

Blanks

Blanks is the concept of creating a stockpile of useable human bodies, which are "alive" but do not have souls. This is tricky, because, normally, if you remove a soul from a living body, the "silver cord" breaks and the body dies. There is internet chatter of underground installations in Nevada where this research is done – reportedly with help from aliens – and where the successful "blanks" are stored. The advantage of blanks is that no special methods are needed to prepare the new body for habitation. Since it has no soul of its own, you just "hop in and drive away." Blanks obtained by chasing a soul out of a living body would violate Universal Law, but blanks obtained by manufacturing a body, which never had a soul, and growing it in an artificial womb would not violate Universal Law. It is doubtful that those doing this research would care either way.

Gods in waiting

At Wright Patterson Air Force Base in Dayton, Ohio, there is a section called "Secure Housing." This is sort of a nursing home for people who have spent their lives in government service and who know too much to be allowed to roam free. Hence the "secure house." The fact that this unit exists is not a secret, but what happens there is. Here is how it works.

The government tells these people that they have been a great service. Everything they have done in their life is then compiled and put on a "microdot." This is stored together with a DNA sample. Then the person is told that "the government thanks them for their service, *but* that the government does not need them any more right now, so they will have to die." However, should the government need them again at some future time, they will be "brought back to life" (using cloning), so that they can serve the state again. Then, when it appears that the person cannot realistically care for himself, they are euthanized. People in this class sign an agreement "never to leave the service of the government," and apparently "never means never."

Activating the "special powers"

Yogis have known for thousands of years about the special powers that humans can develop with practice. These powers are commonly called the Siddhi powers. Yogi masters interested in the spiritual development of their students will caution them to ignore these powers, if by chance they acquire them in the course of their training. This is because becoming absorbed in such special powers makes any further spiritual advancement impossible.

However, if you don't care about spiritual advancement and instead want power, wealth and control over other people, these powers are just the ticket for you. These are the primary Siddhi powers:

1. *Parkaya Pravesh.* Parkaya Pravesh means entering one's soul in the body of some other person. Through this knowledge even a dead body can be brought to life. The need for this Siddhi is largely replaced by the secret body transfer equipment.

2. *Haadi Vidya.* This special power allows a person to neither feel hungry nor thirsty and allows him to remain without eating food or drinking water for several days at a stretch.

3. *Kaadi Vidya.* This special power allows a person to be unaffected by change of seasons, i.e., by summer, winter, rain, etc. A person can sit in the snow or sit in fire and feel no effect.

4. *Madalasa Vidya.* This special power has to do with changing the size of your physical body (shape shifting) from very small to very large.

5. *Vayu Gaman Siddhi.* This special power allows the person to quickly travel from place to place by flying.

6. *Kanakdhara Siddhi.* This special power concerns the ability to acquire great wealth, which is a primary desire of the elite ruling class.

8. *Surya Vigyan.* This is the special power of Alchemy, i.e., transforming one substance into another.

9. *Mrit Sanjivani Vidya.* This is the special power to bring the dead back to life. It has now been replaced by cloning.

10. *Prapti Siddhi.* This is the power to overcome physical distances. It is an altered state where space and time have no effect.

11. *Prakamya Siddhi.* This is the ability to get anything you want. Rulers love this one.

12. *Ishita Siddhi.* This is the ability to defy the laws of nature (physics) and do unexplainable and "impossible" things.

13. *Vashita Siddhi.* This is the ability to put other people under your control (similar to hypnosis). This Siddhi has largely been replaced with effective mind control drugs and methods.

14. *Kamavasayita Siddhi.* This is the ability to get anything you want anywhere you want and is sort of a master power, including many of the other special powers. What politician would not drool at the thought of having this power!

The government has discovered that you can "turn on" these special powers by a combination of hyperbaric oxygen and special ultrasonic frequencies. This makes years of difficult yoga practice unnecessary. It also produces people with amazing power who have no discipline and no regard for humanity.

Aura balancing equipment

The aura is the magnetic field surrounding the human body. Psychics can see auras, and anyone can see them with the help of special filters such as those made with dicyanine dye. Dicyanine dye is an old chemical compound and is not hard to make. However, you may have to find a source outside the United States, because it is supposed to be one of the "secret ingredients" used in U.S. currency and so the government does not want you to have any. (This is really ridiculous considering that the benefits of seeing auras far outweighs some secret component of paper money, but that is how they think.)

The aura relates to the physical body under the "as above, so below" rule. Specifically, a problem in the physical body first appears as a defect in the aura. Since most people can't see the aura, this warning goes unheeded and the physical problem manifests. However, if you were able to see the aura, you could correct a potential problem there and so never have to experience it in the physical. This is what a competent psychic healer is able to do.

The government has now perfected "aura balancing machines," which use sophisticated computers to analyze the magnetic field (aura), compare it to some "perfect reference standard," and make the necessary corrections. Consequently, the gods and other special elite can keep their auras perfect.

This equipment is part of a family of magnetic medical devices. The only member of this family that is public knowledge is the MRI diagnostic device, which was actually an accidental spin off from the original project to develop the aura balancing magnetic device.

When people spend their lives doing bad things – constantly plotting to hurt other people and cultivating hate and the like – the aura is damaged and the person suffers. The elite like to do all these things, but they don't want to suffer the natural consequences of their behavior. Therefore, with periodic use of the aura balancing equipment, they can lead as evil a life as they want and still have a "picture perfect" aura and enjoy excellent health. They have effectively "defeated the law of karma."

Manufacturing geniuses

In past times,when public education actually tried to educate young people, teachers took pride in their work. They knew that not everyone would be an intellectual success, but they also knew that there would be a few outstanding students who would go on to do great things, and this knowledge gave them a sense of job satisfaction.

However, today the government has developed a secret process that will turn any ordinary person into a genius. Part of the process involves drugs that will remove all uric acid from the person's body. This is the key secret. Actually, it is a secret only from the ordinary people of the world. Other governments know how to do this too. In fact, if someone is captured and suspected of being a foreign operative, one of the tests used is to check the uric acid level.

Now that the government can manufacture as many genius kids as it wants whenever it wants, the value of a "naturally occurring genius" has greatly decreased. In fact, a naturally occurring genius would now be considered a potential liability, because he would not be under government control and could possibly develop independent thoughts that could upset the status quo. He would be watched as a potential threat to the national security.

The manufactured geniuses are "contained" in government installations. The kids are not kidnapped, and their parents know where they are. They believe their kids are doing a service to the country. The typical manufactured genius will have several Ph. D. before he becomes a teenager. The kids live on a diet of potato chips, candy bars and soft drinks. No one cares about the future effects this diet might have, because there is no plan to keep the kids beyond the early twenties.

Although the government has all the supercomputers it could possibly want, there are still some problems that only real people can be used to solve. The reason for selecting kids is that, although they can achieve incredible intellectual capacity, they do not have any maturity, common sense or moral values. These are learned qualities that come over time and cannot be instantly "drugged" into someone. The government does not want to see these qualities, because they interfere with work.

For example, if you told mature scientists, *"Go make germs to kill everyone in the world,"* they might have second thoughts about obeying, since, for one thing, they live in the world too. However, if you tell the kids to go do this, they will say, *"Gee! Wee! That sounds like fun! Let's go do it!"* This is why the government uses kids – because the moral component of their personality has not developed yet, and they will freely do projects that mature people will refuse to do.

None of the kids are kept beyond the early twenties. The government cannot kill them, because their parents know where they are. However, it is not known whether the kids gradually return to normal once the special drugs are withdrawn or whether the government uses one of its CEOM (Chemical Erasure Of Memory) drugs on them before they are released.

Clearly, they know things that the government wants kept secret, so it is probable that something is done to them, since the "lack of morality," which the government liked,would now become a liability. The kids would also lack any respect for any non-disclosure agreement they signed.

Because the government can manufacture smart people when it needs them, there is really no longer any need for a strong public education system. Educating "ordinary" people could be a liability, because educated people tend to object to government policies.

Therefore, public education has now been trashed. School is just a place to get a free lunch, buy and sell street drugs, and hook up for sex. There is even a movement to arrange for all school kids to see a psychiatrist who would have the power to force brain damaging drugs on any kid who showed a tendency toward independent thought.

The "Schedule Zero" Drugs

The government arranges controlled drugs into five categories, or "schedules," from I to V. A regular doctor can prescribe from Schedule II to Schedule V. Schedule I are drugs whose names are known (such as LSD), but which you cannot get without a special Schedule I permit that is usually issued to universities and research labs.

However, this does not account for all the available drugs. The cure for AIDS, for example, is kept at all full-service hospitals. It was created at the same time AIDS was created. It is not on Schedule I or any of the schedules. However, it does exist. We have made up the name "Schedule 0" to cover this class of drugs, simply because it sounds logical.

Schedule 0 drugs are available to doctors and others with Q level clearances. In every major hospital at least one of the doctors has a Q clearance. The code name for this doctor is "Doctor Ray." That is not his name, of course, but if you ask to see Dr. Ray, he will come.

Other drugs in Schedule 0 would be the "genius drug" we discussed earlier and the class of brainwashing drugs used to create "Manchurian Candidates" and the like. Also, secret assassination drugs.

"We buy mistakes"

At drug companies, thousands of unique chemical compounds are made, which never existed before. Some become drugs. Some are pure trash and do not do anything. But many others may do weird undesirable things or even kill people. You don't need to throw those new chemicals away, because the government will pay good money for them so it can use them against people it does not like.

Remember, this is a unique chemical that has never existed before. No one knows it has been invented and, therefore, there is no literature available on it and no test for it. Who could wish for a better assassination drug than one with no history, which would be almost impossible to ever isolate and detect.

The Abode of the gods

As a general rule, the government likes privacy. They tend to choose locations where ordinary people will not likely find them. Because most all of the real estate on the Earth is already in use, some creativity is necessary to find places where no one would want to go or where no one can go. Examples of such places would be desolate places like Area 51, inhospitable places like Antarctica, and inaccessible places like the far side of the moon.

However, these places only allow for limited expansion. The solution to this problem is to use the existing real estate of the planet on a lower level, i.e., to build underground cities and installations. This solution provides access to the entire planet – even the water covered regions – as "empty space" for whatever you want to build.

Because of the water-covered regions, there is more real estate available underground than there is on the planet's surface. And ordinary people have no idea that such places exist or are even possible. So, it is just a great place all the way around.

Construction technology

When the idea of moving underground first occurred to the government in the early 1900s, the only technology available was conventional technology like men with shovels and whatever heavy equipment was around at that time.

Later, as the government began to develop its seed knowledge, some very fast and efficient methods became available. The system developed, which is in use currently, involves lasers "pumped" by a small nuclear detonation. This device produces a cylinder shaped tunnel with "smooth as glass" walls that can be made many miles long with one pulse of the laser device. Since the material removed in the excavation is sort of "disintegrated" by this device, excavation can be done at a fairly rapid pace.

Underground transport systems

You may remember, before the age of computers, that stores had vacuum pipes running around so that clerks could put paper documents in cylinders and have them sucked through the pipes to some central office somewhere else. The office could reply through the outgoing pipe.

Because the laser technology makes perfect cylinders that mimic a large pipe, they can be used to transport people and equipment underground at fantastic speeds. A large cylinder, similar to the idea used in stores in the past, forms a car or bus that holds passengers and cargo. One vacuum cylinder goes one way and its companion goes the other way.

The entire planet is now connected by this underground transport system that links all underground cities and underground installations.

Safe terminals

As a general rule, a country protects its air space and its physical borders. However, no one seems to consider the possibility of an attack from underground.

Consequently, the nations that have not yet been taken over and co-opted into the New World Order are easily penetrated by the underground transport system. All that is required is a "safe house" in the target country located where you want to send in agents. This is then tied in with the underground transport system and you can enter and leave the target country whenever you want and the fools never even know you are there.

The underground installations

Underground installations are mainly work places as opposed to underground cities, which are living spaces.

There are underground installations all over the world. However, for our example, we are going to talk about the installation located below Wright Patterson Air Force Base in Dayton,Ohio. This is a huge installation and extends far beyond the physical limits of the base above it and even extends into neighboring states.

This installation is basically an underground office building. Once you get into the underground, you see brightly lit hallways that seem to go on forever. Every so often is an area with electric carts. You grab one and go to wherever you are going and leave it in the closest "cart park" for others to use.

One interesting aspect of this underground office building are the doors to the offices. The doors are about twelve feet tall. Even basketball players don't get that tall. However, it is said that some of the alien races we have business relationships with are almost twelve feet tall so this could be an attempt to accommodate them.

The underground cities

You may have seen TV stories about "secret" underground places for government executives to go in case of some attack. These stories typically show some concrete block room with very uncomfortable looking bunk beds and maybe a crate of tasteless dry food from the 1960s or whatever. Such places may exist, but they are certainly not for anyone at any high level of government. They would laugh at such crap and certainly would not want to stay there. When we say "underground city," we mean "city" with all the associated amenities. Underground cities have houses, open spaces, trees, gardens and, of course, golf courses. They look like any other city, except that they are underground. And they are "Camelot perfect." Remember, "the rain may never fall 'til after sundown…", etc.

Everything in an underground city is state-of-the-art-technology perfect. The air is "manufactured air," which means it is made from stocks of liquefied gasses (nitrogen, oxygen, etc.) that are then mixed in the exact proportions. There is zero pollution. Artificial sunlight creates day and less artificial sunlight creates night. Water can be tapped from natural underground sources. Power is generated from geothermal energy and is essentially unlimited. Local transportation is electric.

The ideal location for underground cities is Africa, because the African continent has essentially no seismic activity. Underground cities are immune to all surface weather problems and are completely safe from any war type event on the surface, however, they do not do too well in an earthquake or similar seismic event. So, they cannot be located in areas of the earth subject to such events.

In the underground cities are located the living quarters for the gods – the permanent residents of the Earth. There are many reasons for the underground such as privacy, secrecy and security. However, the apparent main reason is the anticipation of some future natural disaster, which will end all life on the surface of the planet. The gods, of course, plan to survive such an event. When things quiet down, they can manufacture a new race of people to their specifications and repopulate the surface. Then they can resume business as usual.

Detection of underground cities and installations

When the plan for using the underground was first conceived, it was designed to be a secret place for the elite and the "ordinary" surface people were never to have knowledge of it. However, a problem developed due to the new high-tech equipment in use by the oil exploration industry. This equipment can map the underground, and therefore it can also map the underground cities and installations.

This was discovered by accident in Russia. Russia had allowed some U.S. companies to come look for oil with all of their cute gadgets. At first, they felt that they had found a huge pool of oil. Then they realized that they had actually discovered a gigantic secret underground city. Because this took place in Russia, the event received brief press and was then quietly hushed up.

This creates a problem for the U.S. and the other nations who have underground cities, because they can now be located and mapped. Therefore, all persons who are allowed to possess this equipment must now be watched to make sure that they do not locate and expose the secret underground. Apparently, only oil companies use this equipment. So, since these companies have a close relationship with governments, it should be relatively easy to make sure that no one talks and the secrets of the underground are preserved indefinitely as originally intended.

Sources and Methods

Here we wish to go through some of the basic sources and methods that the government uses to gather information. Sources and methods only work when no one suspects that they exist. So, as we go through these, you will probably be in for some surprises.

Pen Registers

Pen registers are devices, which federal law requires that telephone companies maintain so the government can spy on you. Basically, the pen register is a list of all the phone numbers called from a phone and all the phone numbers of calls received by that phone. Pen registers are maintained on all phones, including public phones.

Phones have been around a long time, and so it has been realized that you can get good information by listening in on calls. That is why we have legislation to prevent this. However, it has only been recently that the Caller ID system became available due to new electronic switching equipment. Originally it was not possible to detect numbers called and received and so no law was written to make logging this information illegal. Before one could be written, the government stepped in and demanded that all calls be logged and that the logs be given to them upon demand.

Let's look at an example of how you might be affected by pen register data. Let's say you are in the front yard watering the grass or something, and someone has car trouble and asks to use the phone to call home for help. You let them use your cordless phone.

Now, say, one of their kids is known to the police for being involved in drugs. The pen register will show a call made from your house to the suspect's house, and therefore you will be put on a secret police watch list as a suspected drug dealer and placed under surveillance. All this will be secret, and you have no way to know it has happened and no way to do anything about it.

To take it further, say, your mate is being considered for a sensitive job. But now the FBI file will have a note about your suspected drug activities, so he won't get the job and will never figure out why, as this is all secret.

This is how the pen register surveillance system works.

Water and drain pipes

When you talk, your voice vibrates things around the house. The NSA (National Security Agency) people have been doing parallel research for years inventing and perfecting unique gadgets that no one knows exist, so they can spy on people.

They are so concerned that no one figures out what they have come up with that employees must agree to die rather than let the secret information be compromised. When they fly their spy planes, the crew understands that they must blow up the plane rather than let some foreign power find the secret equipment. This is usually not necessary, because all of the spy equipment is designed to self-destruct into a pile of useless rubble before anyone could get their hands on it. However, if this cannot be accomplished or accomplished fast enough, the crew understands that they must destroy the plane and themselves with it. This is how serious they are about the revolutionary stuff they have invented, which suggests that it is "really good stuff."

Now, back to the pipes. In this spy method, it is possible to connect to a drainpipe or water pipe in a neighborhood and detect the conversations going on in the houses that the pipes connect to. Secret equipment is able to filter and select so that only one particular house on the pipe network is monitored. This level of sophistication of signal selection and filtering is, of course, one of the secrets. The information has always been there for the taking, but no one had the means to use it.

X-Ray vision

Originally, only Superman had it. Now, we all can have it, because it is for sale. This once secret technique involved equipping an acceptable vehicle (phone trucks are popular) with X-Ray equipment. Then the police would pull up in front of your house, and this equipment would let them see inside without ever knocking. They could see who was home and where they were in the house. If they thought you could resist them, they could just lock on to your position and shoot through the wall and kill you while you were watching TV or whatever. Later, after they trashed your house, they could make up some story that you resisted them.

Now declassified, anyone can buy this stuff. Just go to *www. radarvision.com* and have your credit card ready.

"Stepford Wives"

This is a cute little project involving controlling women with satellites. Since most weird projects are dreamed up by men, they tend to focus more on women than men simply out of the respect of one man for another man as opposed to a "mere woman." Anyway, in this project, a special satellite was to send out signals designed to influence the female brain. Since natural brains are not influenced by satellite signals, it was necessary to give the women brain implants. This was accomplished by arranging for shampoo manufactures to add special liquid crystals to shampoo used by women. Whenever they would wash their hair, some of the liquid crystals would penetrate the scalp and make their way into the brain where they would remain permanently. Once the level of crystals reached a certain concentration, the woman could theoretically be brought under control of the mind control satellite. This is really one of the more creative projects in the mind control collection.

Secret wars

There are many techniques for secret wars. Secret wars have the advantage of deniability. You cannot blame a nation for attacking you, or even trashing and taking over your country, if everything that happens appears to be "an act of god." Let's look at a couple of examples.

ATTACK FROM ABOVE. Suppose you want to secretly attack a country, kill most of its people and then move in and take over the place. You find some migratory bird whose flight habits will cause it to cross the country you want to destroy. You make a contagious designer virus and infect these birds. The virus is designed to be harmless to the birds. However, as the birds fly over the target country and leave their little "birdie duty" along the way, the virus is designed to attack the food crops of the target country and kill them. The people starve and die. Then you move in and take the land. This technique works best with highly populated countries like China, which would simply not have the logistic capability of bringing in enough food fast enough to prevent mass starvation.

ATTACK FROM BELOW. Because the U.S. has a global secret tunnel network, it is no problem to go underneath the country you are going to trash and create some type of devastating earthquake or other severe seismic disturbance that will leave the place in ruins. Of course, "nature" would be blamed.

Incidentally, in the resent tsunami, no news group seemed to mention the tiny island at the center of the tsunami where the U.S. operates a secret base. Strange how they seemed to overlook that fact!

Ultrasonics

If you are in a room with loud music, you will notice that liquid in a glass is vibrating. Also, if you touch the wall or some solid thing, you will feel vibration. So, we know sound waves affect things in their immediate environment. When things in the vicinity of a sound source vibrate, you can analyze these things and reconstruct the sound that caused the vibration.

Now, please refer to the above schematic. There are common devices in almost every home. One is the TV set. In the TV set is a very stable crystal oscillator on a frequency of 15.575 KHz. Some people can hear this high-pitched "whine" coming from the TV. This frequency creates an ultrasonic field that covers your house and extends beyond the walls of your house. When you speak, the sound waves from your voice interact with this known (fixed frequency) field to create an interference pattern. This interference pattern can be detected by spy satellites and, from it, the voices in the room can be reconstructed. This is how the government listens to you in your home, when it wants to.

Now that you know this, you can jam the spy equipment by installing "trashy" ultrasonic generators in your house. Try to find old ultrasonic bug repellants at a flea market or second hand store, because the newer models have been "fixed" so as not to interfere with the spy equipment. This will produce so many random ultrasonic fields that the spy equipment will not be able to lock onto a stable pattern and so will not be able to reconstruct your voice.

Now, say you are in the middle of a lake, fishing with your friend. No one is close to you. You think it is safe to talk. Well, think again. You see, you are most likely wearing an electronic watch. In it is a crystal on a frequency of 32.678 KHz. It is much weaker that the TV set but strong enough to make a field around you and someone close to you. So, spy satellites can tune in on you and hear every word you say. This is basically how the ultrasonic spy system works.

X-Ray Satellites

In case the government also wants to watch you in your home while it is listening to you, it can target your house with one of its X-Ray satellites. Of course, if you live in an old house painted with lead-based paint, they will have a fuzzy picture. Therefore, new laws not only outlaw lead paint, but require the removal of any existing lead paint, so they can get a clear picture.

The system is very selective. For example, if you have a 50-story office building, and you are interested in activities on the 17th floor, you can "tune in" to that floor and exclude the rest of the building.

Clearly, this technology is similar to the new airport scanners that can be adjusted to gradually "strip off your clothes" layer by layer to see if you are hiding anything. The only difference with the satellites would be higher power and more selective focusing ability.

Vendors

Government spies who are constantly slithering around the country killing and otherwise harassing helpless citizens use sophisticated electronic gadgets. This is not the same stuff you can go out and buy at some "spy store." This is stuff that regular people have never seen and have no idea exists. Unfortunately, gadgets brake sometimes and need service. What's a lonely spy to do, far from the home office, should this happen?

Well, fortunately, the government thought of that and established a network of repair centers. These repair centers go by the code name "vendors." So, if your spy stuff needs fixing, you know somewhere locally you can go to get the work done.

Vendors use ordinary garden-variety businesses as "fronts." Flower shops are popular, because nobody would expect anything sinister there. In this case, you would walk into the flower shop and say something like, *"Hi, I have some special trouble with my garden, and I talked to Patty Petunia, and she said you could help me."* Obviously, there is no Patty Petunia, but you have now given the correct code word, and they will let you into the back room where the technicians work, and you can get your stuff fixed or replaced or whatever it takes to get you back in shape to carry on your secret assignment.

Nationwide Doublethink

Now, let's say the "vendor" in the spy fix-it shop needs parts. Well, you need to go to a parts store. But the parts you need are classified, so the catalog is not going to have them. So you say, *"I need some hard to find parts, and Cathy Capacitor said you might have them."* Now that you have said the correct code word, the man behind the counter will hand you a catalog that looks like the regular catalog, but it will be the classified version that will list the secret parts you need. You place your order and pay with your Federal Credit Card.

We have used electronic parts as an example, but the system of "two sets of everything," one for the "ordinary person" and another for the "special" person, applies pretty much to all items and all major suppliers.

There is one "public catalog" and a second "secret catalog," which you can see once you give the correct code-word signal. Because "special" people may live and work side by side with "ordinary" people, there is a whole national language of code words so that the "special" people can get and do the things they need and the "ordinary" people will have no clue as to what is happening.

It could be described as a sort of "cold war" of the secret government against the uninitiated masses, or "the herd" as they are referred to in high circles.

Catholic Confession

This is one of the better-kept secrets. For years now, priests have been passing on to the government anything you tell them in confession that they might find interesting. This is one of the major methods that the government uses to gather information. The Catholic Church has been very cooperative with the government in intelligence, and it could almost be considered a secret arm of the government. Also, because of its power to scare people, it can help the government control people by, for example, telling people that it is a "sin" to try to avoid paying taxes.

As you may have guessed by now, the Catholic Church is a control organization and has nothing at all to do with anything remotely spiritual. It is just a racket to get your money so that its elite members can have a great life without working.

The State of the Art

Here, we wish to briefly go over the real state of the art in science. The "chosen" of the world have now had almost seventy years to evaluate and develop the seed knowledge that they were given for the benefit of all mankind. They have made good progress in the development of this knowledge, although they only use it for their benefit and others' detriment.

Communications

Communications technology is one of the most perfected sciences. Instant global communications are available to anyone who wants to pay the cost, and highly sophisticated global communications systems are available to the military and government.

Today's "secret agents" are supposed to be capable of uninterrupted worldwide communication via a dental implant. Additionally, they are supposed to have a second dental implant for self-destruction. Both are said to be "non removable," whatever that means. The agents are fearless of death because they are promised new bodies if they should die.

This implant technology is also quite effective for the "puppets" the United States installs all over the world as "democratically elected leaders." In the past, when an installed puppet malfunctioned, it required a military invasion to remove the puppet and install a replacement puppet. This can be messy and costly as in the case of Panama and Iraq. Now, with the self-destruct implant technology and communications technology, when a puppet is installed, he will have no choice but to obey orders, because he will be monitored 24 hours a day and can be killed in an instant by remote control if he gets out of line.

Radio transmissions may be cleverly encrypted to prevent the information sent from becoming known. However, the fact that there is some kind of transmission taking place cannot be concealed. Since most people who are concerned with security have equipment to detect that a radio frequency transmission is taking place, we assume that one of the NSA's secrets is that they have discovered some communications technology, which does not use conventional radio frequencies. Such transmissions will not be detectable until someone in the private sector guesses how they work and lives long enough to publish the findings so that the new technology becomes public knowledge.

Physics

Physics is complete. That is, there is no "uncertainty" left as to how things operate. Physics books available to the public end with all sorts of "uncertainty principles" and other assorted unknowns. This is to deliberately keep the average person in ignorance. For those a bit smarter, the so-called "String Theory" seems to be a fairy tale invented to send the curious off in the wrong direction.

All of the mechanics of matter and the Universe have been worked out, tested and verified. There are real "complete" physics books in print, however, you need a top-secret clearance to get your hands on one.

Medicine

There is no known disease that does not have a safe and effective cure. There is no need for you to ever die physically unless you want to. The fact that these treatments and options are not available to you is due to government policy and secrecy. Medicine has become an "industry," as opposed to some kind of "healing art" practiced by dedicated souls sworn to do their best to help you and to never hurt you. This may have once been true, but the only thing that counts today is making money, and the medical industry is very skilled at maximizing its profits.

Like any industry, the medical industry relies on "trade secrets." Trade secrets are things that, if known, would seriously impact the profitability of the trade. For example, an automaker would prefer that you not know the actual cost of production of a vehicle. That way, you will be content to pay the designated price and feel you got a good deal.

The biggest trade secret of the medical industry is that there is really no need for a medical industry. If you had access to the secret vaccinations given to the elite ruling class, you would never get sick. If you had access to top secret cloning technology, you would never die. The only reason you would need medical help would be as a result of some accident or physical injury of some type. If that were the only reason people sought out a doctor, [the doctors] would go broke. Clearly, this is economically unacceptable. Therefore, it is important that people be deliberately allowed to become infected with diseases that are preventable and that new diseases be made in the lab and released to keep people sick and scared of dying so that they constantly run to doctors for "help," all the while not knowing they are actually the cause and not the solution.

Probably the two diseases that the medical industry absolutely loves best are AIDS and cancer. Both are man-made and both have effective cures that are top secret. Drug companies know that they are not allowed to release the real cure without government permission. Of course, there is no economic motivation to do so, because they could no longer profit from suffering people by inventing expensive "cures," which do not work, and selling them at top dollar.

These two diseases together fulfill many of the government's needs and desires. They kill people, which is considered necessary for population control. They boost the economy, because the drug companies and the medical industry can make a fortune selling the helpless people drugs and treatments that don't work and then "standing around" while the poor people slowly die in agony anyway.

The medical industry is extremely wealthy and has loads of lobbyists with bags of money to bribe congress and any regulators to get whatever it wants. What it wants is to stay in business and grow ever richer day by day. So don't expect to see any improvements.

Genetics

Much genetic information is now publicly available. In secret, the state of the art in genetic knowledge and capability is equal or very close to the sophistication of the alien scientists who, tens of thousands years ago, manufactured the bodies we now use. These alien people are the "god" or "gods" referred to in ancient books. There are no books written by the real GOD.

Space and Time Travel

The U.S. has space ships and space travel capability and limited experience in actual space travel. There are limits on where ships from Earth can go due to sanctions for willful and continuing violations of the Universal Laws. However, they sneak out every once and a while and visit uninhabited places or hook up with their little bug and reptile friends. One discovery of interest is that our solar system creates time within its space and other solar systems do the same. The field of control that our sun generates extends out some light years, and larger suns would have larger spheres of influence. A solar system has a factor known in top secret physics as "time pressure." Time pressure determines what elements may freely exist within that system. Therefore, rare elements and elements that can only be man-made and have very short "lives" in our solar system may freely exist and be common in other systems with a different "time pressure." This has been confirmed experimentally by traveling to other solar systems. If Earth's government would clean up its act and respect Universal Laws, we could all enjoy the many new experiences available in other parts of the physical universe, but it appears that is not to be.

Time travel is a reality and has been perfected. The first thing they tried, of course, was to go change the past in the hope of changing the future. It did not work. Einstein predicted that it would not work, and he was right. Changes you may make in the past have no effect at all on the present. So all those science fiction stories are just that – fiction!

A god's Life

Perhaps the most logical way to present this material is to take the theoretical case of a baby born to one of the ruling bloodlines of the Earth. Such a child would have a birthright, or "divine right," to become a god. Let's go through the stages of development of such a child.

Childhood

The young god is like any other naturally born baby. It does not remember its past lives and it is not consciously aware of much of anything at all. The child will, of course, be raised in an environment with every conceivable luxury. During these early years, members of the child's bloodline, as well as those from other bloodlines,will be watching. This is because, should this child be approved for godhood, it will live forever and become a new permanent member of their elite community.

Every once and a while there is an "error." A child develops humane thoughts and strange desires to work to change the world for the better. Obviously, this cannot be tolerated and such a child cannot be allowed to become a god. It may not be harmed, but it will be secretly excommunicated from the elite and will simply not be given the special knowledge of the gods. It will live a normal life and then die and be forgotten. This is just one of those problems when a child is born "naturally."

However, it is more likely that the child will show a tendency towards a desire for power and total disregard for "ordinary" people. Such a healthy sign would mean that, most likely, a new god has been born.

Early Life

Once the child reaches school age, there should be obvious signs as to whether this child will be initiated into the society of gods or not. If yes, the initiation sequences will begin.

Immunizations

The parents will order what is code-named a "health kit" for the child. This consists of several bottles of liquid, which the child will be told to drink or which will be gotten into the child somehow like mixing with food. The child will then be immunized for life against all known diseases, including all special diseases, which the government has created and released (like population control viruses such as AIDS) or that have been prepared and may be released in the future. Beyond this point, the child will never get sick. Child may or may not be told about this at the present time.

Special school

Obviously, child will never go to anything remotely close to a "public" school. Child is a future ruler of the world and is above all of those ordinary "trash" people. Child will go to a special school where other elite kids go and will develop friendships with other children, many of which may also be "young gods."

Attitude

Child will be watched for its attitude and method of handling interpersonal relationships. It is a future ruler and, as such,must show no weakness or compassion. If a male child has a problem with a girl and kills her (like the Kennedys do), this would be a positive sign that he is "real god material," having demonstrated total ruthlessness and total disregard for human life. Special god training would probably be started immediately. As for the girl, suitable women are a "secondary inferior creation," so who cares? Bury her and forget it.

Young adult life

Now the young god in training is ready to start its special training, which will place it forever above the ordinary person. Parents may take young adult to one of the secret libraries where the true history of the United States and the world is recorded. History books available to the general public are creative works of fiction at best.

In the secret libraries, child will learn about the FRUS (Foreign Relations of the United States) books, which contain the true history of the country. Child can read, for example, the secret indictment against President John F. Kennedy that was used to justify his murder. If child is into "spacey" stuff, he can read the true report of the Roswell UFO incident, which is listed in FRUS as a legitimate event.

Augmented college years

Obviously, child will be accepted and will attend one of the Ivy League colleges. Child could go to Yale and get to join Skull and Bones, but other colleges will do just as well. If child elects science as a major, the textbooks used in publicly accessible colleges will be insufficient, because all state-of-the-art science is secret. Therefore, the book companies, which print watered down and obsolete stuff for the "ordinary" student, also print correct state-of-the-art books for those with proper clearances. For example, an ordinary person obtaining a Ph. D. degree in physics would be left with a bunch of "uncertainty principles" and the general feeling that "we really don't know anything." Actually, physics is a complete science, and there is no "uncertainty" left at all. So, the classified books would cover subjects like "Temporal Science" and go through the classified Einstein equations and thoroughly explain everything.

Adult Life

By now the child has been confirmed as "god material" and will be instructed as to its special status and told that it will live here and participate in the ruling of the world forever. It will probably want to join some of the classic insider groups, such as the Bilderbergers or the Illuminati, so it can have friends who are on the same level.

Marriage

It will have been explained to the young god by this time that the elite bloodline must be preserved as it has been for thousands of years. Parents may have pre-selected an appropriate mate or suggested several approved possibilities. Love is irrelevant. Production of genetically correct children to preserve the bloodline is the primary purpose.

Should the young god totally reject this idea and choose a "commoner," it could be stripped of its future rights as a god and excommunicated from the elite circle it now enjoys.

It would be unusual for the young god to make such a choice, because by now it knows it is destined to live forever with every possible luxury, if it conforms to the accepted rules of conduct.

Occupation

The "elders" will decide how best to use the new god. It might be made into a Senator, or even be selected to do some time as a U.S. President. Generally, U.S. Presidents are always from one of the ruling bloodlines of the world and are pre-selected by a committee of "elders" (for want of a better word). Once the committee has selected someone, the press programs the general population in such a way that they elect the selected person. There have been errors in the programming process, notably in the case of President Kennedy, who was not supposed to win. Such errors, however, are corrected.

"Retirement"

As an older and wiser god, your work for your first lifetime as a god is coming to a close. You will have some retirement years where you will not have an active job. During these years, you will want to visit the secret underground cities and pick out some permanent accommodations where you will live when you are fitted with your new body. You will also get to meet the "residents" who will eagerly anticipate the day that you will join them.

What to do with the wife

As a general rule, the wives of gods do not need to know about the underground or that their husbands intend to live forever. There are plenty of young healthy females in the underground for recreation, and it would be a drag to be stuck forever with the same woman, even if she was fitted with a new young body. Therefore, wives usually do not have any knowledge about this.

The classic example is the retired CIA boss who went out fishing one day and went missing "floating down the stream." Later, the boat "floated back" with his dead body. Clearly, he was picked up by his buddies, taken to the underground and fitted with his new body. Then the "empty shell" was floated back so his wife could have closure. She had no clue.

Life in Your Second Body

You have several choices in selecting a new body. You can choose a new identical body (clone). You can choose to take someone's body away from them using the body swap machine (anyone joining the armed forces must sign over their physical body to the government, and therefore the government has the legal right to do anything it wants to that body, including removing the spirit from it and allowing it to be used by another spirit).

However, you will probably want to select a "manufactured" or "remanufactured" body. All natural bodies have some defects due to years of "tinkering" and radiation damage from the 1950s, when they were popping nukes everywhere for tests. A "remanufactured" body has been checked by genetic engineers for imperfections and all of them have been found and corrected. Such a body would guarantee you a "physically carefree" second lifetime.

Your new life in the underground

As a new god, you really do not have to do anything at all. The work of all the "ordinary" people of the world is for your benefit. You are entitled by "divine right" to anything you want. You have access to all available knowledge and technology. You can even go visit other planets or take trips in time if you want. Anything you desire will be provided.

However, once you settle in, since you plan to be here forever, you will most likely want to choose some activity to avoid becoming totally bored. There are many committees and study groups you can join where the future of the planet is debated and decided. As you develop seniority, which may not happen until you are on your third body or so, you may play a part in the ruling council of elders, which is the actual negative core group that controls this planet. This would be your ultimate level of advancement within the world of the gods. Only the most evil and sinister can hope to reach this level. To do so is considered the ultimate accomplishment.

Managing the Herd

The United Nations refers to the collective peoples of the world as "the herd." They speak of such things as "how can we decrease the size of the herd" (population control), and so on. So, as a member of "the herd," you may be interested in some basic ways that are used to "manage you."

The Cage You Live In

You live in a cage. You were born in this cage, and you will die in this cage just like some pet bird, or chipmunk, or whatever. You may not have noticed this, because the cage is rather large. However, it is a cage just as well.

Let's say you live in a major city and let's now look at the forces that control your life.

First, you are by no means a free person, because you must "voluntarily" sell yourself into slavery in order to get your fiat (faith-based) paper money so you can buy food to stay alive and some place to protect you from the elements.

The things you feel you know to be true were programmed into you by state controlled education and are reinforced every day by state controlled media.

"You are what you eat," and the only thing that there is to eat is processed food containing god-knows-what additives, which you consume every day, and you have no clue what they are or how they affect you.

In a large city, the air you must breathe may be sprayed with special chemicals designed to influence your behavior psychologically or damage you physically by causing cancer or some other dreaded disease.

In your neighborhood is a paid government informer who knows you and who may even be one of your friends.

Your phone is tapped and all your calls are recorded and saved for a specified amount of time. If you are "interesting," these records are saved permanently.

X-Ray satellites can watch you inside your home at any time. This is why lead paint was outlawed.

You cannot cross an international boundary without permission, and some international boundaries are off-limits. In the future, you will need your National Identity Card and Internal Passport to leave your city and to cross checkpoints within your city. Your vehicle will electronically report its position to the government so that your movements can be logged.

If you have a cell phone, be advised that it is not only reporting your position, but it can be remotely turned on so that it transmits your conversations with whomever you are talking. Turning the cell phone off will not stop this. If you want privacy, you must remove the battery. Otherwise, it can be secretly turned on and used as a listening device.

Above you is space. You know it is there, but you have no idea what activities take place there and you cannot go there.

Below you is the underground. You don't even know it exists.

This is your situation – "love it," because you "cannot leave."

Population Control

The world population is "adjusted," based upon the needs of the ruling masters. As technology increases, less people are needed to do the slave jobs, because machines now do these jobs. Therefore, the "surplus people" need to be eliminated. Also, specific sub-groups of the general population are evaluated for their work potential or "output" as slaves. "Lazy" groups of people are scheduled for elimination first. In keeping with this scheme, the long-range plan is to eliminate the black race first, and then to consider elimination of Latinos, because they like their "siestas" and don't work as hard as other groups do.

AIDS was originally invented to eliminate the black race and specifically to depopulate Africa. Later, the military suggested that it could be used to get rid of gay people, which it has never really approved of. So agents were sent to the gay areas of California to give out free hepatitis shots laced with AIDS to eliminate the gays.

In general, the medical profession has the duty to see that you "die appropriately," i.e., that you do not live too long after retirement, because to do so will cost the government money. In an interesting news report from some years back it was noted that when all of the doctors in a small town went out on strike for some reason, the death rate actually declined.

The government is always looking at new population-control methods. Early on, they designed "food additives," which were supposed to sterilize women. The additives failed to sterilize women, but did succeed in giving them cancer, which then forced them to accept treatments that would sterilize them. So the project was considered a success.

The government likes cancer as a population control agent. After years of research to "cure cancer," cancer rates are actually rising. Common sense should tell you that this is a farce. No one is trying to cure cancer. Cancer research is for the purpose of finding new ways to make people come down with cancer for population control. It is also a big money-maker for the medical industry, as is AIDS.

Street Drugs

Let's talk a bit about street drugs. You have, no doubt, heard the argument that it is really the government that is behind street drugs to, among other reasons, acquire money to finance its black projects. So let's apply a little common sense to this situation and see what we can learn.

First, there are theoretically bands of international drug smugglers – dangerous, desperate and fearless against all authority – dedicated to penetrating national borders to deliver drugs to their faithful users. OK, hold that thought.

Now, if gangs of smugglers operate under the law of supply and demand, we should see a supply of a drug if there is a corresponding demand for it. Obviously, these people are in this game for money, and so if there is a profit to be made, they should be there. So far, so good. There is a good supply of heroin and, actually, since the U.S. took over Afghanistan and made it into one of its "satellites," the purity of street heroin has reached an all-time high. No problem finding marihuana hash or crack either.

Now suppose you want LSD. Well, street LSD is not just hard to find – it is *impossible* to find. It does not exist. There is no pure LSD available on the street in the United States (however, you can buy it for about 50 bucks per milligram if you have a Schedule I DEA permit).

Now, this is strange, because if the international cartels have no problem finding acres to plant poppies and acres to plant pot, why can't they find a few acres to plant rye, which will then become infected with ergot, which is the key ingredient in LSD.

To make LSD, all you need is ergot and the common chemical reagent diethylamine, together with some basic lab equipment. It is easier to make LSD than to go through the various stages you need to do to turn opium into morphine and then heroin.

So why don't these desperate dangerous dealers provide LSD as they do heroin? There is certainly a demand. It is a high profit item and easy to smuggle – only one milligram needed for a super "trip." So why is it not there?

We argue from the circumstantial evidence that the U.S. does have the power to reduce the availability of a street drug to zero, if it wants to. Therefore, we conclude that the reason street drugs exist in this country is because the government wants them to exist – wants people to use them and be damaged and addicted – and most likely makes a profit somehow from this whole operation.

If the government was not in total control of what is available on the street, we would surely see a supply of LSD. However, we do not.

Incidentally, you probably know that regular cigarettes cause cancer, but did you know that the government, which subsidizes tobacco farmers, also provides those farmers with radioactive waste that they are required to plow into their tobacco fields?

Go figure!

Effective Use

The purpose of the social order is to extract energy from the slave class for the use of the god class. This is usually rated in terms of money. If the social order is losing money on some person or group, they are a drain on the system and therefore do not have the right to exist.

In times past, a dead human body had little or no value. However, today a freshly dead human body, properly chopped up and packaged, is worth about $100,000.00, mainly to the transplant industry. Therefore, if the estimated "value" of a person to society is less than $100,000.00, it is to the financial benefit of society to slaughter that person and sell it for spare parts.

Additionally, there are other uses for "nonproductive" citizens that do not involve killing them right away.

Missing and exploited children

Well, the title is correct – they are missing *and* they are exploited, but the details should surprise you!

Runaways are a drain on society. They annoy tourists and use up social services. Also, they have some "attractive qualities." For one thing, no one who knows them or cares about them knows where they are. This means that, should they "disappear," no one will be the wiser.

If you are an attractive young girl, or if you fall into the category of a "cute, supple, young boy," you will probably be used for a sex slave. Otherwise, you will be used for spare parts. (If you are or plan to be a runaway, you should seriously consider maintaining contact with some mainstream person who can tell your parents if contact is lost. This will not help you, but it will give your parents some closure, because they will know that you are never coming back.)

Here is how we play this game. Kids and others who are secluded to be slaughtered for parts are stored in Mexico. Obviously, they are not told that they are waiting to be killed. Exactly what story they are given is not known, but it would be something to "keep them quiet and cooperative" while they are "waiting." When the call comes in for something for which there is a tissue- type match "in stock," the appropriate person is slaughtered and the desired parts are shipped out.

If you are cute and are selected for a sex slave, you will be taken to a government brainwashing center in the U.S. for "processing." Processing is similar to the *Clockwork Orange* movie. You will be given drugs to make you susceptible to suggestion and then shown films. For the purpose of sex slavery, these will be sex films to train you into what to do and to program you to like and desire what you are trained to do. If the programming is successful, you will be put to work.

Sex slaves that are captured by "private industry" are stored and trained in Mexico before being shipped to their destination. Private industry does not have the special methods available to governments and so uses various "crude but effective" methods.

Sex has always been popular in diplomatic circles. The classic erotic film *Emmanuelle* (Sylvia Kristel and Alain Cuny) is based on the diary of a diplomat's wife and is essentially a true story (you must be over 18 to watch it). Nothing has changed today. When you entertain foreign dignitaries or even heads of state, you try to provide them with appropriate entertainment. Some like girls. Some like boys. Some may like both. It is diplomatic courtesy to make these things available. Young runaways are generally in good health, and after you "clean them up" and "program them," they make excellent and vibrant sex slaves.

Additionally, the brainwashing system can be applied to other special uses, when necessary, like making people into "Manchurian Candidates" and the like. It appears to be the films and not the drugs that affect the brainwashing. The drugs only create susceptibility to suggestion.

Division Five

Division Five is supposed to be a special division of the FBI whose job is to murder U.S. citizens who are deemed to be a threat to the national security. There are supposed to be about 12 different groups, all called "Division Five" for compartmentalization, and members of one group think that they are the "only Division Five" and don't know about the other 11 or so "Division Fives." Every day thousands of U.S. citizens are murdered by these people.

The state of consciousness of the "average American" is really a belief system. This belief system is carefully designed to maximize productivity. Since it is imaginary, with no real relationship to any "concrete reality," it is quite fragile and any "disturbance" could seriously affect production quotas. Consequently, it must be constantly "maintained" by eliminating any source that could cause "disillusionment" and cause people to "lose their belief." Division Five ensures the stability of the belief system by systematically eliminating any dissenting source that could disturb the delicate status quo.

Some of the cases where a Division Five agent would be dispatched to kill you would be: *(1)* if you discovered *a cure for AIDS*; *(2)* if you discovered *a cure for cancer*; *(3)* if you had *physical evidence of a UFO*. These are just a few examples of things that would guarantee your immediate death.

In case you are wondering about "bad people," like terrorists and general criminals, the government actually likes these people. If it were not for them, it would not be possible to scare people into voluntarily giving up their freedoms and accepting a police state. It is the honest people seeking to help and uplift humanity that the government fears, not the criminals.

Incidentally, so-called "organized crime" has now been incorporated into the secret structure of the government, because it can get away with stuff that the "real government" cannot. The two are now secretly co-opted together and are fast friends.

Retention

Human bodies are alive because they have Souls. Souls choose to come to this place, because they feel it will accelerate their development. Earth is considered a challenge, and any Soul who successfully escapes from Earth is shown great respect, because it is such a difficult lifetime to do.

However, as conditions on Earth worsen for the average person, new Souls may choose not to come here. They have that right. In such a case, if the quantity of human bodies being produced is greater than the quantity of human Souls who choose to come here, nature will assign an animal soul to the unused body rather than let it die and go to waste. This is called a "minion incarnation."

As conditions on Earth systematically worsen, the leaders worry that they may run out of human Souls to "play god to" and boss around, because human Souls will refuse to come here. Therefore, they have come up with various schemes to prevent the human Souls, which are already here, from ever escaping.

Psychic interference devices

Psychic interference devices are denial devices designed to prevent natural psychics from using their abilities. They mainly consist of radio frequency interference patterns broadcast over specific frequencies known to affect humans.

Spiritual interference devices

Spiritual interference devices are designed to prevent the Souls of the dead from leaving the sphere of influence of the Earth rulers and, instead, forcing them to reincarnate on the Earth. The classic "tunnel with the light" that many claim to see when near death, is supposed to be a mechanical "Soul trap" designed to "suck up Souls" and then hold them and force them back to Earth in a new body, whether they want to come back or not. It is supposed to be of alien design and is discussed on the *TRUFAX* web site. Please see *www. trufax.org* for more specific details.

Operation of a spiritual interference device is one of the highest violations of Spiritual and Universal Law.

Playtime

We have now established the basics of how the world operates and discussed who is pulling the strings and the various techniques they have developed and use. Now we want to discuss everyday activities,which we call "playtime." You don't want to get bored with your life as a god, so you need to do stuff to keep occupied. Since you have no power beyond the planet Earth, your "play" will consist of projects directed at (or against) the general surface population that you hold hostage.

Testing Operating Systems

When the Earth rulers decided to abuse the seed knowledge, they realized that finally they had within their power the tools to create what they had always dreamed of – a one-world absolute dictatorship, which we commonly call the New World Order.

The question then arose as to what would be the best way to manage such a system to achieve desired results. Since this was to be a world of slave labor, the desired result was productivity – how to get the absolute most out of the slave before it drops dead from abuse.

A series of "test governments," or operating systems, were tried. For example, the United States created and financed the Soviet Union and still secretly controls it today. It was used to test the concept of an overt dictatorship where there was no doubt that you were a slave and would be tortured or killed if you resisted. This technique worked to a point. However, terrified people were found to be less productive due to the stress and fear under which they lived.

The United States tested a system of "democratic illusion," which it called "democracy." A real democracy would be unthinkable, because you would lose control of your slaves if they really had self-determination. So the solution was to create a system where the people were constantly told how free they were and how it was they who voted and therefore determined their fate, and then secretly control things from behind the scenes.

This worked great, and so it was decided that the most efficient operating system for maximum productivity from the slaves is "democracy." Consequently, the non-democratic systems that still exist in the world are being gradually converted to democratic systems, now that the testing is complete.

The democratic system coupled with false future hopes produces very high productivity. You get people all sexed up telling them how free they are and then promise them great retirements and all kinds of good stuff "off in the future." Then, when the future comes, you tell the suckers, *"Sorry, social security is broke,"* and, *"Sorry, someone stole your pension money,"* and so on. By then, the slave is old and you don't need it any more, so you don't care what it thinks or what happens to it. You got your productivity, so screw the stupid slave for believing your lies. Turn your attention to conning the young generation of slaves.

North Korea – the Incubator for Future Slaves

The people in South Korea are from the same genetic stock as those in North Korea. So we know they have the potential to be very productive, since their brothers and sisters in the south are. The people in the north have been beaten down just about as much as it is possible to do. They have literally abandoned all hope.

This is great, because, when the United States takes over North Korea and installs a puppet leader and proclaims it to be an "emerging democracy," U.S. corporations can move in and get work out of the people there for essentially nothing. If you have a group of people living on grass and mud and you drive in as the "liberator" with a truck full of Twinkies, the people will bow down and gladly do whatever you want. You won't even have to pay them a salary – just give them decent food and promise you won't kill them if they do not meet the production quota. In the future, the U.S. corporations are going to have a ball there, and the local people will be happy and "glad to be a free democracy."

"A Time to Build Up, a Time to Tear Down"

Eventually, a group of people gets too comfortable. They demand more money. They demand more benefits. They refuse to do some jobs at all. Americans are now like this. That is why all the factories have to move out of the country.

However, gradually other countries learn too. Their people start asking for rights, benefits and more money. To make sure you do not run out of slaves, there must be some kind of recycling campaign.

When a society gets too affluent, you need to do something to it to "beat it down" so that you can later "raise it up" and exploit the people in the process. You can arrange some kind of revolution, "natural" disaster, plague or some such scheme to trash the society. Then, when all hope is beaten out of the people, you come in and "rescue" them and put them to work in factories for a fraction of the wages that you had to pay them before they were "recycled."

Depopulation of Africa

Africa is a special place. It has essentially no seismic activity. For this reason, the World Control Directorate is located there – underground, of course.

However, the surface of Africa is pretty too. Unfortunately, it has been determined by the rulers of Earth that the native people simply cannot be adapted to the New World Order. Therefore, the decision has been made to kill them all. This will create fresh real estate, which can then be occupied and developed by "approved" people. It is similar to the occupation of America, which was already occupied by the Native Americans. Try to find them now.

Henry Kissinger, who reportedly signed the order to begin systematically infecting the African people with the AIDS virus that U.S. scientists had manufactured, is said to have called this process "cleaning out" certain parts of the world. It is like taking a "chemical mop" and just mopping up the unwanted people and putting them out for the trash.

Anyway, despite being infected with AIDS, the African people continued to live, so then the "fast kill" designer virus Ebola was used, but they survived that too.

Then it was decided to send in agent provocateurs to start civil wars everywhere and let the people kill each other. Additionally,whenever no one was looking, CIA agents would fly around and drop poison on whoever looked like they were not being effectively killed by the other methods. The process is ongoing, but eventually there will be no Africans left in Africa and the U.S. corporations can move in and develop the land as they see fit.

When the Federation Comes Calling

If you were in some position of responsibility on another planet and you got word that some "Federation" from the planet Earth was on the way to pay you a visit, you would want to get every weapon you could find and blast them out of the sky. You would know that these people were not "seeking out new life," but were rather "seeking to conquer" new life, colonize the planet and turn the native population into slaves. In short, they are bad news. No civilized world would want people from Earth, under its present directors, to come anywhere near them. No advanced society would want to touch Earth with a ten-light-year pole!

Persuasion

Let's say that you are the leader of some country. One day, a representative from the United States comes calling:

You: What do you want?

U.S.: I have come to ask you to turn your country over to us and to become a puppet of the United States.

You: You must be crazy. I am the supreme leader here, and our country does not need you, and our people are happy. I will never do such a thing!

U.S.: Well, that is understandable. However, I would like to invite you to come visit the U.S. for a few days as our guest. You have our oath under the principles of diplomatic immunity that no harm will come to you, and we would really like to show you some things that we promise you will find interesting.

You: OK, I will come, but my position will never change.

U.S.: Fine.

(In the U.S., you enter an elevator for an unusually long ride that appears to be downward.)

You: Where am I?

U.S.: You are in one of our underground cities. This city is my home. Everything is perfect here. The air is absolutely pure and all natural elements are totally computer-controlled to maximum perfection.

You: This is incredible.

U.S.: Yes, quite an achievement. We have been building them for years now and we have them all over the world. But you must be tired now from your trip. As it is late, let me get you some quarters assigned and we can talk in the morning. Would you like some girls from our diplomatic recreation division for the night?

You: Well, OK!

U.S.: (Walkie-talkie.) 257 and 092, report. (Two girls show up.) Go with this man. Anything he wants. Understood?

Girls: Yes, Sir.

U.S.: Have a good night. See you in the morning.

(The next morning.)

U.S.: Good morning. Had a pleasant night?

You: Sure did. Your girls are great. We can't get our slave girls to do some of the stuff yours do, even when we threaten to kill them. How do you do it?

U.S.: We use chemical persuasion, very efficient. Most of these girls were young runaways. They were a burden on our society. Now we capture them and send them to processing. They turn out as you see them and are now useful.

You: What happens when they get older?

U.S.: We send them for recycling. They are stored until someone needs a spare part – liver, heart, whatever – and then, they are used to provide it. Very efficient reuse of a biological unit, and most of them are in excellent health. What would you like for breakfast?

You: That guy over there… I know him, but he died ten years ago!

U.S.: Why don't you go enjoy breakfast with your "dead" friend and then we can talk.

(After breakfast.)

U.S.: You see, I invited you here so that you could see these things for yourself. We are gods. This is where we live. We are totally protected from all outside forces. I died 16 years ago. This is my second body. When it wears out, I will get another one, and another, forever. Your friend you just had breakfast with is one of us. From our underground bases and cities we control all activities on the surface of this planet.

You: You do not control my country. We are a proud and sovereign nation.

U.S.: Well, that is what we need to discuss. Here is our proposition. If you will secretly turn control of your country over to us, we will promise you entrance into our community of gods. You will become a god like us and live forever and have every conceivable luxury. If, however, you reject our proposal, we will take your country by force. We already have agents in your country. We can release deadly viruses and cause mass death and panic. Our agents can arrange a civil war. Eventually, after we trash your country, we will get a UN resolution and invade it directly and make it one of our satellites. You will most likely be killed. Certainly, you know of our power and you know you cannot resist us militarily. However, none of this will be necessary if you voluntarily submit to us... So, what is your answer? Do you agree to become our puppet and, in exchange, be allowed to become a god and join us and live forever, or do you choose to resist us and be killed when we come take your country by force?

What would you say, if you were put in this position?

Sanctions and Consequences

When we began and discussed the seed knowledge, we noted that it was not a "strings-free gift." It was designed for the benefit of humanity and not to enslave humanity as has been done. Since the Earth leaders seem to have no ethics or regard for the agreements they make, sanctions and corrective measures have now become necessary.

In the case of sophisticated spiritual criminals, simply putting them to death has no effect because they immediately grab a new body and continue on as if nothing had happened. Therefore, the ultimate penalty of AID is used in these cases. In this penalty, the Soul of the accused is stripped of all its bodies (physical, astral, causal and mental) and is then dumped into the void or zone of darkness, which separates the created universes from the pure spiritual worlds. Here, the helpless soul wanders around lost forever. There is no return from the AID penalty. Since the "gods" underground will face this penalty when they are captured, they essentially have nothing to lose and will therefore take any steps they can think of to escape judgment.

The general human population of the Earth, although handicapped by genetics that have been damaged and tinkered with throughout the years, are still capable of spiritual evolution. It is a fundamental violation of the Universal Laws, therefore, to design a system to prevent Earth humans from spiritually evolving. This is what the Earth rulers have done. Such a situation cannot be allowed to continue indefinitely.

If you offer loaded guns to children and then the kids go running around killing people and each other, common sense would say that you have to accept responsibility for this. Similarly, the civilizations that attempted to help the Earth people by giving them advanced technology have a responsibility, now that this knowledge has been misused, to correct the situation.

The Earth is already under sanctions that prohibit it from any contact with advanced civilizations. That is why the only space activities you see are things close to home like making space stations and such.

Earth has made a few "friends" from other worlds, but they are not human and are fundamentally inferior to humans. The Insectoids (commonly called the Gray People) and the Reptilian races do not desire spiritual advancement, because they are not capable of spiritual advancement. It is not part of their makeup. Therefore, they spend their time seeking power and military conquest.

It is ridiculous to have a spiritually capable race (humans) being dominated by advanced bugs and lizards together with evil humans who have no place to go, because they are wanted criminals for Universal Law violations, and so hide underground in the Earth to avoid capture. However, this is the current situation.

For those of you who live on the surface of the Earth, you need to know that you do not live under the rule of any type of "government." You live under a cult. You cannot join this cult or even meet its members, because they are all safely hidden underground. This cult controls your life, and it controls your life to your detriment. If you expect any relief from your situation in the future, you must at the very least become aware of the true nature of your situation. Otherwise, those of you who cannot leave the planet Earth, will continue to be "playthings of the gods."

Published in issue 7 of The Dot Connector magazine (January-February 2010).

Notes

I GIVE CARTE BLANCHE TO MY SOUL

CLIMATEGATE: A CRIME AGAINST HUMANITY

1. climate-skeptic.com/2009/11/yet-more-stuff-we-always-suspected-but-its-nice-to-have-proof.html
2. dakotapolitics.com/blogPost.asp?PostId=21393
3. abcnews.go.com/US/TenWays/story?id=3719791
4. whatreallyhappened.com/pearl/www.geocities.com/Pentagon/6315/pearl.html
5. whatreallyhappened.com/McCollum/index.html
6. whatreallyhappened.com/SH.html
7. whatreallyhappened.com/wrharticles/rancho/crash/twa/tonkin.html
8. whatreallyhappened.com/wrharticles/blair.doc
9. whitehouse.gov/news/releases/2003/02/20030205-1.html#44
10. news.bbc.co.uk/1/hi/world/middle_east/404896.stm
11. thememoryhole.org/war/yt-misleading.htm
12. thinkandask.com/news/colinpowell.html
13. spacetoday.org/Satellites/YugoWarSats.html

14. cnn.com/2003/US/03/07/sprj.irq.un.transcript.elbaradei/
15. whatreallyhappened.com/wrharticles/rapture.html
16. networkworld.com/archive/1999/55717_02-22-1999.html
17. youtube.com/watch?v=0lgzz-L7GFg
18. oism.org/pproject/s33p36.htm#Message5974
19. whatreallyhappened.com/wrharticles/Anthropocentric Global Warming
20, 21. surfacestations.org/odd_sites.htm
22. abcnews.go.com/US/TenWays/story?id=3719791
23. newsbusters.org/node/11879
24. eclipptv.com/viewVideo.php?video_id=6933
25. whatreallyhappened.com/wrharticles/globalwarming2.html
26. See graphics at: whatreallyhappened.com/wrharticles/climategate.php
27. eastangliaemails.com/emails.php?eid=544&filename=1120593115.txt
28. whatreallyhappened.com/images/snowoct09/index.html
29. noworldsystem.com/2009/12/11/50-of-the-u-s-is-covered-in-snow-already
30. whatreallyhappened.com/wrharticles/Paul Hudson, BBC weatherman who in October was sent Climategate emails has been gagged by the BBC.
31. abcnews.go.com/US/TenWays/story?id=3719791

THE MARIJUANA CONSPIRACY

© Doug Yurchey, 2009.

SINISTER FORCES IN AMERICAN POLITICAL WITCHCRAFT

© Kerry Cassidy and Bill Ryan, 2009.

WERE HUMANS CREATED AS SLAVES?

© Michael Tellinger, 2006.

BEYOND EXOPOLITICS

© Mado, 2009.

1. *Personocracy* – the state of consciousness typical of a human being holding full power over her own life. It is possible only when a person has given priority to the soul over the ego.

2. *Adam* means "cattle" in Sumerian and Akkadian.

3. *Idessa* – the name of the Supreme Being inherent to all that exists. She is both the Creative Spirit and the created matter. The word was coined by Ghis from the words "identity" (*id*) and "goddess" (*-dess*). Even if Idessa is both feminine and masculine, the final "*a*" is meant to feminize the word so as to respect the order of creation: *feminine principle* (spirit/soul) → *masculine principle* (mental, vital and physical matter).

PROJECT BLUE BEAM

© Serge Monast, 1994.

1. http://i.am/jah/evolut.htm
2. http://educate-yourself.org/cn/uscconcentrationcamps28jun01.shtml
3. http://educate-yourself.org/cn/chinaandorganhavesting31mar06.shtml
4. http://educate-yourself.org/ps/psrcresmokestackshawaii31jul01.shtml

AWAKEN IN THE NOW

© Colin Bondi, 2009.

PLAYTHINGS OF THE GODS

© Walter C. Vetsch, 2005-2009.

About the authors

Paul Bondarovski

An independent French journalist of Russian origin. After 30 years as reporter, editor, designer and art director in the mainstream press, including a Top Ten French illustrated monthly, he started, in January 2009, his own international independent magazine, the *Dot Connector* (*www.thedotconnector.org*).

Colin Bondi

Colin Bondi is a counselor, healer and writer living in Portland, Oregon. His counseling work is based on simple in the moment presence and its ability to initiate healing by helping step out of the mental stories and thought patterns that are at the root of most suffering. He practices energy work, including Reiki, and uses this to help remove blockages and allow energy to flow naturally. He can be reached at *dreamercolin@yahoo.com*, or at his website: *www.awakeninthenow.com*. For appointment scheduling (in Portland, Oregon only) please call 503-863-9862.

Kerry Cassidy

Kerry Lynn Cassidy has a BA in English with graduate work in Sociology, an MBA certificate from the UCLA Anderson Graduate School of Management, and was competitively selected to attend a year of film school at the UCLA Extension Short Fiction Film Program as one of their first "hyphenates": a writer-director-producer. After 19 years in Hollywood working for major studios and independent companies in production, development and new media, she has written a number of screenplays, acquired an option on the movie rights to the *Wingmakers* (*wingmakers.com*) story in 2003, and started work on her own UFO documentary in 2005. Since 2006, she devotes all her time to Project Camelot (*www.projectcamelot.org*).

Peter Levenda

Peter Levenda is an author and researcher, primarily in occult history. He appeared in the TNT documentary, *Faces of Evil*, in his role as an expert on Nazi history with special regard to the occult and esoteric practices. He has also appeared on the History Channel special, *Nazi Prophecies*. Perhaps best known for his book *Unholy Aliance: A History of the Nazi Involvment with the Occult* (1994; second edition, 2002, ISBN: 0826414095), Peter Levenda is the author of eight books, including the trilogy *Sinister Forces* (2005-2006; ISBN: 0975290622, 0975290630, and 0975290649). He lives in Miami, Florida. His website is at: *www.sinisterforces.info*.

Mado

Since her best friend's probable ET abduction when she was fourteen, Mado has been reading everything she could find about the subject. She discovered that the New World Order was not only related to all the spheres of society, but was also deeply linked to exopolitics. She finally managed to connect all the dots when she discovered Ghis' *personocratic* approach. Her excitement grew when she realized that Aurobindo and The Mother (Mirra Alfassa) had been on the same path and explained the coming of the idessic being in great detail. She now spends her time giving conferences and writing with Ghis the popular series called *Personocratia's Booklets*. She lives in Quebec, Canada, and can be reached, in English and French, at: *personocratia101@gmail.com*, or at the websites: *www.personocratia.com* and *www.jemesouviensdequijesuis.com*.

Serge Monast (1945-1996)

The Canadian investigative journalist Serge Monast had faithfully exposed the New World Order agenda for over a decade. His children were home-schooled, so the Canadian authorities abducted his eight year old daughter, then his seven year old son, on the pretext that the parents were "abusing them emotionally" by stopping them going to a state school. The father was arrested, and spent the night in jail. Next day, December 5, 1996, at home, he died of a "heart attack." Within a week, another Canadian journalist, also researching Project Blue Beam, died of a "heart attack" while visiting Ireland. Neither had a history of heart disease. Serge Monast wrote to his friends that he had been threatened many times, especially when he had started to collect the revelations concerning Project Blue Beam secretely or anonymously given to him by contrite politicians, military and intelligence people.

Michael Rivero

Michael Rivero was born in Boston and spent his childhood in New Hampshire. In 1993, he launched *WhatReallyHappened.com* website (initially called *Rancho Runamukka*), which today is among the Top Ten ranked daily political news sites on the Internet. He also runs the *What Really Happened* radio show on GCN and regularly speaks on the *Alex Jones Show*.

Bill Ryan

Bill Ryan has a BSc in Mathematics with Physics and Psychology (Bristol University, UK, 1974), and followed this with a brief stint in teaching. For 27 years he was a management consultant specializing in personal and team development, leadership training and executive coaching. Major long-term clients included BAe (Systems) Ltd (formerly British Aerospace), Hewlett-Packard, and PricewaterhouseCoopers. In November 2005 he inaugurated the *Project Serpo* website (*www.serpo.org*), the report of an alleged disclosure, in stages, of a US-alien exchange program, which took place half-a-century ago. While he had been interested in UFOs, free energy research and alternative medicine (he is trained as a kinesiologist) for over 30 years, his first contact with the UFO community at large occurred after establishing the Serpo website. He resigned his management consultancy post in May 2006 and now devotes all his time to *Project Camelot* (*www.projectcamelot.org*).

Michael Tellinger

Michael Tellinger describes himself as a 'closet scientist' and 'serial entrepreneur' with a passion for the cosmos and pushing the boundaries of knowledge. He is a writer and performer by heart – scientist by calling. Michael graduated from Wits University in 1983 with a degree in Pharmacy. He worked for Cannon Films in Los Angeles as a sound designer and editor, has written and recorded a multitude of musical projects. As a writer in advertising he received a Clio award in New York and had his own weekly show on Cape Talk radio. *Slave Species of god* is his first published non-fiction book (Associated Pub Group, 2005. ISBN: 1920070133). His website: *www.slavespecies.com*.

Walter C. Vetsch

Walter C. Vetsch was born in 1947 in Louisiana, with a gift that he himself defines as the *"unlearned knowledge."* Many of us, over the years, generally acquire a degree of wisdom which cannot be learned in schools. When we pass away, this knowledge dissolves in the universal consciousness, so when we're back here in our next incarnation, we usually have to start everything from scratch. This was not the case of Walter. From his earliest years, he knew exactly what "reality" really was, how it worked, and what were the forces that made it work. He knew that this knowledge was true, and the best cofirmation of it was that when, in the end of the 1960s, he decided to expose this knowledge in a book, those same forces violently opposed to it. *"There is a federal program in the U.S. for psychiatric screening of children starting school,"* Walter says. *"They are looking for any evidence of psychic abilities and can brain damage the kids before they realize their potential."* Walter was taken to a psychicatric hospital, where for seven years "doctors" tried to do their best (worst?), using torture and drugs, to erase the "unlearned knowledge" from his memory. There were other children like him in the hospital, all died in consequence of this kind of "treatment," Walter was the only one to survive. In 1972, he wrote his first book, Plan Theory. It didn't mean the government left him alone. They killed his children, brain damaged and sterilized his girlfriend, all to make sure his bloodline "stops here." (See the detailed report on this, about 300 pages, at *www.louisianastate-hospitals.com.*) *"All that I write,"* Walter says, *"is based on the material I was able to bring through from before I was born here. This is what triggered the people who look for that sort of stuff, persons with 'unlearned knowledge,' which could upset a system where knowledge is controlled."* His website is at: *3108.info*.

Doug Yurchey

Doug Yurchey (born in Pittsburgh, PA, in 1951) is a writer, artist and inventor. While operating an art gallery, he encountered Katrina Satler, a super psychic who inspired him to dedicate his life to solving great mysteries. His research led him to scientific genius Nikola Tesla. Because of his study and understanding of Tesla, Yurchey has literally rewritten history. The idea that our ancestors were technologically superior is a vital theme that he currently promotes. In 1990, Doug was hired as a background artist on the Simpsons TV Show, and later has become a successful Internet writer with 10,000 Google listings. He has lectured at Carnegie Mellon University and California State in Northridge. Doug Yurchey is the author of a 300-page book, *The Atlantis Tesla Connection*, which he is literally giving away at *www.world-mysteries.com* on a signed CD-ROM for a symbolic price of $10.00, including its case, cover art and p&p. His forthcoming book, *TRYUNE*, is a fantasy about events that happened long before the age of Atlantis. The synopsis for the manuscript is available at *www.world-mysteries.com*.

Made in the USA
Lexington, KY
30 July 2011